THE FIGHTIN' 589TH

THE FIGHTIN' 589TH

By Col. Thomas P. Kelly, Jr.,
F.A. Ret.
AND
Lt. Col. Elliott Goldstein
F.A. Ret.

1stBooks – rev. 01/04/01

TABLE OF CONTENTS

CHAPTER XIII
The Battle of Parker's Crossroads Begins

CHAPTER XIV
The Battle Heats Up

CHAPTER XVII
Aftermath of the Battle-Brutality
(Soldiers Who Were Captured and Became
Prisoners of War in Stalags or Work Camps)

CHAPTER XVIII
Aftermath of the Battle-Cruelty
(Officers Who Were Captured and Became Prisoners
of War in Oflags)

P R O L O G U E

By Colonel Thomas P. Kelly, Jr., F.A. Ret.

Great feats of army units, like those of armadas of the Navy and wings of the Air Force, are frequently the product of chance--circumstances that confront the unit and require that it exert superhuman effort to survive and to accomplish its mission. Of course, a unit so challenged may fail or may succeed--may break and run or stand and fight--and history records many examples of both responses. While the odds faced by the unit frequently determine its behavior under fire, the chances of survival are not always controlling.

The character of the men composing the unit and the inculcation of values during their training will, more often than not, determine their response to life-threatening tactics of the enemy. But, a unit's reaction is rarely predictable, and may vary with the disposition of the opposing force when the threat arises. Frequently, the conduct of one individual, not necessarily the commander, will decide the outcome. But in the final analysis, it is the depth of determination in each individual soldier, his commitment to the cause for which he has laid his life on the line, that will win the skirmish, or the battle, or the war.

It was this determination and this commitment that distinguished the men of the 589'" Field Artillery

xi

Battalion of the 106'" Infantry Division of the United States Army in World War II. The Battalion received its baptism of enemy fire in the "Battle of the Bulge", the last great offensive of the German Army on any front, inspired by Adolph Hitler and designed by his Chief of Staff, General Jodl, to advance through Belgium to Antwerp, driving a wedge between the British 21st Army Group and the American Armies to the south. The victorious Germans could then force the surrender of the British Armies and negotiate an armistice with the Americans that would permit them to turn all of their forces to the east and defeat Russia. To Hitler's distorted mind, this result seemed not only possible, but attainable. And there was a period of about thirty days when the Allies were not certain of the outcome.

This massive engagement was called the Battle of the Bulge because the attack by three German armies against a very thinly held sector of the American eastern front created a bulge covering hundreds of square kilometers of the sovereign territory of four nations (Germany, Belgium, Luxembourg and France) that had been overrun by the Allies in late 1944, and that had been envisioned by the American armies as the launching pad for a final drive to end the War.

The Battle was finally won by the Allies early in February, 1945, but it was initiated by the Germans on December 16, 1944, a very cold, overcast day that emulated a long series of days that had afflicted western Germany and eastern France in late 1944 (and were to continue to do so). The advance of German forces on that date and the succeeding three days led to the worst single-day catastrophe from the standpoint of casualties in the entire military history of the United States, a day upon which the 106 Infantry Division suffered more than 8,500 casualties (the exact number will never be known) or over 60% of its total strength. And the vast majority of these losses occurred in the relatively small triangle between Bleialf and Auw, Germany, and Schönberg, Belgium, and in an area that did not exceed three square kilometers (approximately two square miles).[1]

In addition to the casualties in the 106th Division there were losses by the armored forces, tank destroyers, anti-aircraft, engineers, medical and other troops supporting the Division, and by many other American units in numerous sectors of the battlefield, including the 99th Infantry Division in line north of the 106th, and the 28th Infantry Division, south of the 106th. The day of the final

---

[1] See map on appendix i.

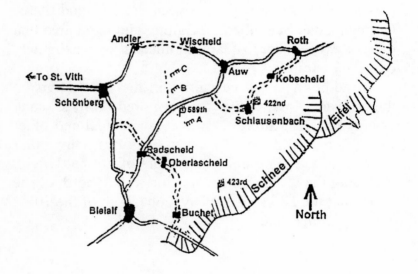

appendix i

massive surrender of 106th Division forces was December 19, 1944, a day that changed the course of many thousands of lives.

Of course, all of these facts are the subject matter of many histories written closer to the date of their occurrence than any commentary I might add as a footnote at this time. But it occurred to me as I read accounts of the Battle of the Bulge on its 50th Anniversary, that there was an insight that was missing in all of the histories and narratives that I have read, particularly regarding the heavy losses suffered by the 422nd and 423rd Combat Teams of the 106th Infantry Division, because the historians and chroniclers were not there. And I suddenly realized that I was in an unique position in that I had not only spent the days and nights of December 16-19 in or near that fatal triangle, but I was undoubtedly the only person alive now or then who had spent many hours with each of those units on December 19, and who had discussed their overwhelming dilemmas with their respective Commanding Officers. Perhaps because of my close association with the principal actors in the tragedies of that day, and the previous three days, I can relate an additional basis for understanding what occurred, and why. And I can, with certainty, recount the actions and exploits of the 589th Field Artillery Battalion in the early stages of the Battle.

As the Commander and one of the leaders of that Battalion, I should like to think that those of us in positions of leadership so disposed the minds of the approximately 500 men under our command that each of them truly and fully believed in the justice of our cause, and were able to demonstrate total devotion to that belief on the field of battle. But the fact is that all Americans knew that we were protecting our homes and our way of life from the efforts of a marauding egomaniac who was determined to dominate the peoples of the earth, and fanatical devotion to such a cause was not difficult to arouse.

In any event, it is an historical fact that the men of the 589th Field Artillery Battalion, to the man, demonstrated courage far beyond the call of duty in the Battle of the Bulge, even though they were part of a "green" division with only one week of pseudo combat experience before the Germans attacked frontally and on both flanks of the Division with three armies on December 16, 1944. What followed that attack in the fatal triangle and thereafter is at the heart, and is the reason for, this story.

Because I was surrendered to the Germans by my combat team (infantry regimental) commander after the first four days of the Battle, I have called upon other members of the Battalion to memorialize its final participation, including one of the most gallant stands in the face of overwhelming odds in the history of American arms. This was an engagement that became known as the "Battle of Parker's Crossroads" for which the 589th was awarded both the French and the Belgian Croix de Guerre, and many participants received Bronze and Silver stars.

To bring you this most stimulating part of the story, I have relied upon Major Elliott Goldstein, the Battalion Executive Officer, who shared command of the remnant of the 589th defending the Crossroads with the late Major Arthur C. Parker, the Battalion S-3. Major Goldstein has persuaded many participants in the Battle and the defense of the Crossroads to write their recollections, and then correlated their accounts (to the extent that they could be reconciled without conflicts and with minimum confusion. I should add that any accurate account of the Battle will necessarily reflect its prevalent confusion, which is the nature of combat.)

Writing during a period in which our nation has enjoyed decades of peace (interrupted only by Desert Storm, a conflict of commendable brevity), one must realize that readers may well be militarily illiterate. In order that the life and death of a military unit will be understood, I shall first relate how, in time of war, a civilian becomes a soldier and is then joined with many other civilians to form, and become a member of, a unit. Then I shall recount how, after the birth of a unit, it is educated, trained and brought to maturity in order that it can accomplish its mission, never self-ordained, but always determined and directed by higher authority or by the enemy. Finally, I shall describe how units, regardless of size, must learn to work with other units, but without losing their individuality or the individuality of each member of the unit, upon whom ultimate victory depends.

The reader presumably will also be without knowledge of what it meant to be a prisoner of war of the Germans and an inmate of one of their prison camps. I and others (notably my Battery B Commander, Captain Arthur C. Brown) shall supply a first-hand account of this experience, and shall even describe how one can extricate oneself from the onus of POW status. Finally, the reader may not know how anyone can be lucky enough to survive all of this and live to write about it fifty-five years later; and neither do I.

PROLOGUE

By Lt. Colonel Elliott Goldstein. F.A. Ret

Many veterans of the Battle of the Bulge put away their memories as they tried to reintegrate themselves into civilian life. I was one of them. My memories were painful, and I saw no reason to revive them. My former commanding officer, then Lieutenant Colonel Thomas P. Kelly Jr., published in *The Cub* of T*he Golden Lion* an account of the opening battle in the Ardennes, and it brought back many memories that I had put into my subconscious.

I was a major, assigned as Colonel Kelly's executive officer, and I was struck by the fact after reading his article that we had been in two different wars after the first day. He thus encouraged me to write my story. With help I was able to secure a copy of the after action report that I prepared following the battle, which was eventually filed in the War Department Archives. But when I commenced work, I realized that my memories had faded. At that time John P. Kline, editor of *The Cub,* asked for comments on an article entitled "Parker's Crossroads, The Alamo Defense"; the article and the comments were published in *The Cub,* (volume 3, number 3, pp. 15-36). I thought that if all of those who participated in *The Cub* article pooled their recollections, we could paint the picture of the action as viewed from the ground by those who fought in it. Of course, we could not enlist everyone, but the twelve who joined in this effort provided a story more complete than any previous account of the Battle at Parker's Crossroads. What I planned as an account of my recollections became more vivid and developed into a much greater work, a realistic picture of combat as seen by each individual. I acted as the scrivener who put the work together, but each of the persons mentioned below is, with me, equally the author of this history:

Calvin V. Abbott	John C. Rain
Barney M. Alford, Jr.	John R. Schaffner
John F. Gatens	Earl A. Scott
Charles P. Jacelon	Bernard C. Strohmier
Harold J. Kuizema	Frank Tacker
Randolph C. Pierson	Eldon L. Miedema

In addition, we have quoted from the reminiscences of Captain Arthur C. Brown, now deceased, and from a letter of Lieutenant Colonel (Ret.) Olin F. Brewster, which was published with the article, "Parker's Crossroads: The Alamo Defense", for which we thank him. We are also indebted to Robert C. Ringer, then a first lieutenant commanding the Train of the 591st Field Artillery, for his report on the eleven men from Service Battery of the 590th Field Artillery who joined us at Parker's Crossroads. We are deeply indebted to the late Francis H. Aspinwall, the battalion historian, who spent many years researching and writing the history of the 589th Field Artillery Battalion. This work was relied upon by John R. Schaffner as a source of additional information for use in composing his narrative.

We also thank John P. Kline, editor of *The Cub,* for his help and encouragement. And special thanks are due Ms. Asta Moore, my administrative assistant, who assembled the work, proofread and edited it. This could not have been done without her.

One of the most extraordinary engagements of World War II was the blocking action by a part of the 589th Field Artillery Battalion, 106th Infantry Division, at Baraque de Fraiture, Belgium, also called Parker's Crossroads. The battered remnants of a field artillery battalion, with no infantry training and only the combat experience gained when they were attacked at the beginning of the German advance into Belgium, delayed the advance of a German Army Corps for five days, permitting the Allies to regroup and stop the German advance short of its objective. Pooling their memories to give an accurate account of what transpired, these members of the 589th hope to show what American soldiers can accomplish under the most dire of circumstances.

After a relatively brief staging period in England, the 589th Field Artillery Battalion, with the remainder of the 422th Infantry Combat Team, units of the 106th Infantry Division, landed at Rouen, France on December 5, 1944, combat loaded. The average age of the enlisted men was twenty-one. After one day in bivouac, the battalion moved across France and Belgium into Germany and went into position a few miles east of St. Vith, Belgium. Having never before been in combat, the officers and men of the battalion had no sure knowledge of what to expect, or whether their training would produce victory when they eventually engaged in combat with the enemy. Nor were they able to improve a great deal on their learning during the eight days in position before the Germans attacked.

On December 16, 1944, the German Army launched its last major attack on the Allied Forces. Driven back into the fatherland, the Germans had regrouped and prepared a drive designed to cut the Allied Forces in Belgium off from their supply lines and to drive a wedge between the British armies and those of the Americans, forcing the British to surrender or evacuate and the Americans to come to terms, granting an armistice that would permit the Germans to turn east against Russia. The path the Germans chose, through Belgium, was one that they had followed before, through the Ardennes, along the Schnee Eifel and on into the mountainous and wooded region of Belgium. The area they chose to attack was a twenty-two mile front defended by the 106th Infantry Division, a division with no real combat experience, which relieved the 2nd Infantry Division and occupied its positions just inside Germany in segments of the Siegfried line. The commander of the 106th Infantry Division was told that the area was a "quiet zone" in which there would be little action, since the Germans were expected to attack in the area to the north near Cologne and Coblenz. However, the intelligence on which this assumption was based was erroneous, as the 106th Division would soon discover.

In combat--except for those in a headquarters working with maps--the center of the war is where the individual is located. His observations are limited by what he can see and hear. In this work veterans of the 589th Field Artillery Battalion have put their recollections together to preserve an account of what transpired in their sector during the Battle of the Bulge. The narratives are set out in chronological order, with each of the narrators identified. In addition, excerpts from a privately published memoir by the late Captain Arthur C. Brown are included.

CHAPTER I

How Ordinary People, Even Lawyers, Can Become Soldiers

Thomas P. Kelly, Jr.

It is well known to many, and not exactly a confession, that I never wanted to be a professional soldier, and did not intend to become one. Ever since the age of three years, when I was able to understand what my father did to keep us well fed, dry and happy, I wanted to be a lawyer. It is true that I attended the University of Florida, where Reserve Officers Training Corps (ROTC) was a required course for first and second year students. But in Florida, where the Great Depression started in 1927 with the collapse of the real estate boom, in the year 1930 one attended the tuition-free, public university or none at all (and less than 10% of high school graduates were able to do so).

It is also true that I elected to take the last two years of the ROTC course, qualifying students for a commission as a second lieutenant, but only because there was a small stipend payable to those who did so and my two jobs, waiting on tables at a boarding house and supervising the gatemen and ushers at football games, only served to make ends meet, and didn't take care of week ends.

And I confess that as a Reserve Corps second lieutenant of Field Artillery (F.A.) I opted to join the 116th Field Artillery Regiment of the Florida National

1

Guard, with headquarters near my home in Tampa, but again only because my weekly drills produced more cash than my monthly salary of $35.00 (plus room and board) as an associate in my father's law practice.

So it was venality, or more accurately financial necessity, that caused me to be in a unit that was federalized on November 25, 1940 (four months to the day after my marriage) for what was then projected as one year of active duty. But as the events of the year 1941 unfolded, it became clear to all of us that one year was just the beginning, and that we were honor bound to serve our country in what would become the largest and most devastating military conflagration the world has ever known.

The 116th Field Artillery Regiment was assigned for training to Camp Blanding, a post still under construction in north central Florida, with the balance of the 51st Division of the Florida National Guard. My best friend, First Lieutenant Baya M. Harrison, who was also recently married, and I were able to rent a tiny house on Keystone Lake for the duration. We flipped for choice of bedrooms and I won, selecting the larger by several inches. Both bedrooms consisted of a double bed and a very narrow passage around it to a closet that was 2 feet by 5 feet with one hanger bar and two hooks. The dimensions of the rest of the house were comparable. We were comfortable and happy (also we were young and newly married).

The most interesting experience that the year 1941 produced was enrollment in the Battery Officers Course at the School of Fire, Fort Sill, Oklahoma. It was there that a new technique for the employment of

2

artillery had been devised and put into practice, using forward observers (FOs) and a fire direction center (FDC). The FOs were not restricted to observation posts (OPs) but with a jeep and a radio operator could accompany the infantry into areas of combat in the front lines and respond to calls for artillery fire by platoon and squad leaders. And the FDC could receive radio directives from the FOs or OPs and convert them into data for the firing batteries, bringing down three battery volleys (12 guns or howitzers) on a target within minutes. It should be noted that no other army in the world had a comparable method or plan for the employment of artillery for maximum effectiveness.

During the better part of three months that my wife and I spent in a little garage apartment on the outskirts of Lawton, Oklahoma, I studied the science of artillery as I had never done before. In addition to fire direction there were logistics, time fuses, survey, nighttime occupation of position, creeping barrages, time on target (TOT) and astronomy (the latter science was wasted on me because there was not a single night in combat during which we could see a star, or even a single day when we could see the sun). It was all very fascinating; besides in the evening there was absolutely nothing to do in the little town of Lawton, and the chill, spring winds screaming over the barren plains and past our second floor windows were not conducive to quiet walks in the moonlight.

Upon federalization of the 116th, I had been promoted to the rank of First Lieutenant and assigned as Executive Officer of Battery B, a job I enjoyed because the Battery Executive is in charge of firing the guns (pieces), and that's where the action is (we still had the French 75 mm. gun in lieu of the 105 mm. M1 howitzer, to be issued later). Upon my return to Camp Blanding from Fort Sill, I was reassigned as a staff officer in Headquarters Battery of the 1st Battalion in order that I could teach all of the officers in the Battalion what I had learned at the School of Fire. This assignment carried with it a promotion to the rank of Captain. But I didn't enjoy being on staff and longed to return to Battery B. When the Commander of that Battery was reassigned, I requested the Regimental Commander, Colonel Homer W. Hesterly, to transfer me to that position. After giving the matter his usual thorough consideration, the Colonel granted my request. I was determined to make Battery B the best damn' 75 mm. gun battery in the whole world. As the reader shall see, I didn't have sufficient time in place to complete that undertaking.

Before November 25, 1941, the one year of active duty was indefinitely extended, except for those who could demonstrate that continued service would result in hardship. Of the many who could have made such a showing, very few applied. The War, including the German invasion of Russia and the U-boat attacks on shipping in the Atlantic, was heating up. Japan was enlarging its war against China and was extending its conquests to the south. A delegation sent by the Japanese government to Washington was making no concessions. The fireside chats broadcast by President Roosevelt were becoming more and more grim and foreboding. American industry was accelerating its shift to production of the materials of war. Still, what

4

happened on the morning of December 7, 1941, to change the lives of virtually all of the people on earth, came as a surprise, shocking the people of America and awakening them to a new and unwelcome reality.

CHAPTER II

War Becomes the Ultimate Enterprise

Thomas P. Kelly, Jr.

On the afternoon of December 7, 1941, my wife and I were resting in our tiny Camp Blanding home and looking forward to one of our rare visits with our families in Tampa on the following day. The occasion was a trip by the entire 116th Field Artillery to celebrate and participate in the dedication of its future home at Tampa's Benjamin Field, where a huge new building had been constructed to be named in honor of the Regiment's Commander, Homer W. Hesterly Armory.

I had turned on our portable radio and suddenly the program was interrupted by an announcement. It was a very brief statement to the effect that there had been a bombing of military installations at Pearl Harbor in Hawaii by planes suspected of being Japanese. Before darkness fell, however, we had heard enough to know that America was at war with one, and probably both, of the world's most formidable military powers; a war that would require the most strenuous efforts and the most demanding sacrifices ever asked of the American people, with no assurance of ultimate victory.

It was too late to cancel the trip to Tampa and the planned celebration, but the dress parade was dismal and depressed, and the speeches seemed hollow and superficial. Everyone was much more concerned about the news from the Island of Oahu and from the Capitol in Washington. But the Headquarters of the Army in Washington and of the 51st Division were very busy.

That night, at the Homer W. Hesterly Armory, I and other battery commanders received sealed orders with instructions not to open them until we had proceeded back to Camp Blanding at dawn on the next morning and had fully prepared our batteries for a change of station, leaving on the following morning. Those instructions were faithfully carried out and when I opened my sealed orders at Blanding on the next day, I learned that Battery B was to proceed to the City of Key West at dawn on the following day (a distance in excess of five hundred miles) where I was to report to a Lieutenant Colonel Putnam, Commander of the Coast Guard Station, who would become my Commanding Officer. This order was also faithfully executed, but not without many hardships and a few crippled vehicles that had to be towed into Key West.

Our new home (bivouac area) in Key West was an abandoned parking lot where we were to pitch our pup tents and one larger tent for the Battery Headquarters. The parking lot had never been paved, but 1st Sergeant Peter Grahn reported to me that the ground would not permit the driving of tent pegs and I remembered that the Florida Keys are coral islands, largely without a layer of top soil. It was necessary for me to buy an electric drill in order to imbed the pegs for every tent in the Battery.

The mission of Battery B on Key West was to oppose and prevent the landing of German troops from

U-boats, and to destroy any of those undersea denizens approaching the island. The day after our arrival, we began the arduous task of mounting our four French 75 mm. (a bore of about 3 inches) guns on elevated parapets lining the shores and at the points designated by Lieutenant Colonel Putnam. It seemed strange and even ludicrous to me that each designated gun position was between two 12 inch coast guard cannons with elaborate equipment for loading and sighting. And there were plenty of projectiles and powder bags under the casements. Why had we come more than 500 miles to position our four tiny little guns among at least a dozen of these behemothic engines of destruction? Finally, my commanding officer answered this question with three whispered words, "No firing pins."

My executive officer, 1st Lieutenant Oscar D. Howell, and I moved with our wives into a furnished home, one of the most beautiful on the island. It was owned by a descendant of one of the founders of Key West, who happened to be on an extensive voyage out of the country. My wife, who was to become a most accomplished and tenacious camp follower, discovered the vacancy when she arrived in response to my summons, two days after my arrival. She and her wire-haired terrier, Patches, and I settled down to what promised to be an idyllic existence: a commanding officer who had his own problems and who did not want to be bothered with mine; a beautiful, young wife with her watch dog; faithful followers who had nothing to do off duty except fish from the seawall and

9

who brought us either fish or stone crabs almost every day. War was beginning to look very peaceful.

We saw a few submarines a mile or more offshore and even fired several rounds at them, but I doubt that we scored any hits. I devised a plan for the defense of the island which was approved by my commanding officer and would have been effective to destroy any landing party, by day or by night. But then the end came to this subtropical vacation in the form of an order from the War Department: it seems that my grades in the Battery Officers Course were good enough to merit my being called back to the School of Fire as one of the first wave of new instructors to accommodate the rapidly increasing body of students for a greatly expanding army.

Even though this meant the end of what had proved to be an extended second honeymoon, I was glad to receive these tidings of things to come. Fort Sill was the world center of learning in the field artillery business, and if I was to become a professional soldier (and World War II was no place for amateur commanders) I might as well learn at the fount. But there were also unpleasant and unwelcome aspects of the assignment. I would probably never see the 116th Field Artillery and my beloved Battery B again, because instructors at Fort Sill rarely were returned to their units (if they were successful, as I intended to be). And Oklahoma was far from home and my other family, although my brother had been transferred to the Army Air Force at his request and would be trained as a pilot in Texas. My sister was married to an Air Force officer who was stationed in Minnesota. But so far so good; for all of this I was grateful.   Wars frequently do more harm to families than to force their members temporarily to part.

CHAPTER III

Becoming a Professional Artilleryman

Thomas P. Kelly, Jr.

My wife and I drove to Oklahoma and reached Fort Sill around the first of February. I was fortunate to arrive in time to be assigned to quarters on the Post (my friend, Captain Harrison, was in the second wave of instructors and had to rent in town). My assignment in the Battery Officers Course was instruction in gunnery, but this involved almost every aspect of field artillery, which can be defined as the science of hitting enemy targets with projectiles, or their fragments or contents, fired from mobile artillery pieces (guns or howitzers). The instruction was not all in classrooms; there were field exercises using "School Troops", including occupation of position by a firing battery, firing for effect on targets located by survey and by observation, adjusted by the use of both OP and FO methods. Since the latter exercises could be classified as a sport (the targets were not alive), it was for me more fun than work.

Early in the year 1942, the standard infantry division began undergoing a change. The old "square" division, including regiments of artillery, was abandoned in favor of the "triangular" division, the basic elements of which were three combat teams, consisting of a regiment of infantry and a battalion of artillery armed with 105 mm. howitzers, one battalion

13

of artillery equipped with 155 mm. howitzers in general support, and special troops (engineers, ordinance, signal, quartermaster, etc.). This change was undoubtedly both timely and combat effective; the divisions became much more streamlined, cohesive and controllable, making communications, movement and deployment much more rapid and responsive.

As this change in the structure of the army division was being implemented, there was also the draft and a flood of volunteers rapidly increasing the number of recruits in basic training, and requiring the creation of new schools and units to which they could be assigned. This, of course, created a need for additional officers of all ranks, accelerating promotions of most members of the officers' corps and creating a need for thousands of officers in the lower rankings. The solution was obvious: enlisted men deemed to be officer material in existing units and among the recruits were singled out and sent to schools where they could attend crash courses to qualify them as 2nd Lieutenants. At least 5 men from my Battery B went through the Officers Training Course at Fort Sill while I was there. (I would have selected all of them as fully qualified.) The Infantry School at Fort Bending, Georgia, was equally busy, as were the armored and special services training schools.

The next logical and necessary step in building an army that could fight (and win) in both Europe and the Pacific, was to allocate the graduates of basic training camps and officers training courses to new divisions, where they could be trained in specialties and welded together as fighting units. Thus was the "New

Division Officer Course" established at Fort Sill and other military training schools throughout the nation. In the course at Fort Sill a "cadre" of artillery officers to be assigned to each new division was given a crash course in gunnery and tactics encompassing the latest developments in field artillery maneuver and employment. These officers had not seen the men they were to command, who were being assembled at the Post where the division would have at least a year of training as a unit.

The duty of instruction in the New Division Officer Course at Fort Sill was assumed by the faculty of the "Advanced Course", the "think tank" of primarily West Point graduates who had heretofore instructed field officers (majors, lieutenant colonels and "full" colonels). But when cadres of the new divisions began to arrive, it became necessary to increase, and ultimately to triple, the size of the faculty. One of this distinguished group, a West Point lieutenant colonel, arrived unannounced in my classroom one morning while I was teaching a course in leadership and military education of enlisted personnel. Although I didn't realize the purpose of his presence, after he declined to participate I decided to make his visit worth his while. I used some material that I had been concocting and organizing but had not yet presented to a class. I thought it came out pretty well, and apparently so did the West Pointer; three days later I received an order transferring me to the faculty of the Advanced Course.

Fort Sill was the hottest and the coldest place I had ever experienced. There were ten consecutive days when the temperature exceeded 110° F. in the summer of 1942, and four consecutive days when it was below 5° F. in the winter of 1942-43. It would have helped then if I had known that the latter experience was preparing me for the most miserable of all winters two years hence. But when you are preparing men for combat, facing the most destructive mechanisms of death ever devised, weather cannot be a factor. Regardless of weather and all other deterrents, we completed our courses and exercises on schedule, just as our students were expected to do in Europe and the Pacific.

When we had first arrived at Fort Sill, my wife, Jean, and I were advised that we would probably be there for a year and it seemed a good interlude in which to start our family. Our daughter, Carla Jean, was born on November 11, 1942. After we returned to the Post from a Christmas leave, I was advised that I would probably be assigned to one of the new divisions in a staff capacity (I had then been promoted to the rank of major) and knowing that every new division is in training for at least a year, Jean and I were equally expedient in producing a son, Thomas Paine, III, on November 12, 1943. We were then in training for transfer overseas, and I realized there would be no further immediate prospects for increasing our family. But with two children one year apart, I knew Jean would be as busy as I would be, for the duration.

CHAPTER IV

Vicissitudes in Preparing for War

Thomas P. Kelly, Jr.

In 1943, the New Division Officer Course at Fort Sill was receiving and training at least one division artillery officers cadre each month, and all of us on the faculty were extremely busy all day and on many all night exercises. When we were told that the next cadre to arrive would be the 106th Infantry Division artillery officers, I was not impressed, until I was informed that I had been designated as the Division Artillery S-3, and would be leaving Fort Sill with the cadre. I was happy to be assigned to many of the cadre's classes and instruction sessions, and all of its field exercises.

The Commander of the Division Artillery was to be a Brigadier General Brock, a product of the National Guard who had army experience in some capacity during World War I. It was apparent to us as instructors that he would have made a satisfactory infantry commander, but that he was totally deficient in understanding modern artillery, technique and employment. His apparent Executive Officer, Colonel Malin Craig (whose father of the same name had served as Chief of Staff of the Army a few years earlier), was of a different stripe. Literally raised in the Army, there was no military challenge that he could not meet or crises that he could not handle. In the ensuing two years we were to become very close friends, as were his wife and mine.

Although I was assigned to attend every field exercise of the 106th Infantry Division Artillery officer cadre, mercifully I was not required to critique their performance. (Each field exercise was followed by a critique during which one of the instructors pointed out errors in the plans and orders of the officers involved as the final step of the learning process.) I would have been a very unpopular Division Artillery S-3 if this duty had fallen to me. But on the whole, this cadre was no worse, and perhaps a little better, than the average.

The 106th Infantry Division was assigned for training to Fort Jackson, an old and well established army post just outside of Columbia, South Carolina. The official activation date was March 15, 1943, but we were not fully assembled and able to begin active training until some time in April. Jean and I were able to find a little house to rent between the City and the Post, and took some consolation from the fact that we were at least 500 miles closer to home than we were in Oklahoma.

As S-3 of the Division Artillery, with promotion to the rank of Lieutenant Colonel, I was the "Plans and Training Officer", responsible for a regimen of training for the four battalions of artillery in the Division. Of course, I had a lot of help. Army Ground Forces Headquarters in Washington prescribed schedules, regimens, courses, tests, field exercises and other activities that kept the units busy from reveille to retreat, and the officers from retreat to taps. My function was to provide supervision, conduct officer classes and to communicate orders from the Division Artillery Commander and his Executive Officer to the four artillery battalion Commanders.

Major General Alan W. Jones was the Division Commanding General, Brigadier General Herbert T. Perrin was his assistant, and Colonel William C. Baker was his Chief of Staff. The principal units of the Division were three combat commands consisting of a regiment of infantry supported by a battalion of artillery as follows:

> 422nd Infantry Regiment (422nd)
> 589th Field Artillery Battalion (589th)
> 423rd Infantry Regiment (423rd)
> 590th Field Artillery Battalion (590th)
> 424th Infantry Regiment (424th)
> 591stField Artillery Battalion (591st)

In addition, the 592nd Field Artillery Battalion (592nd), equipped with 155 mm. howitzers, was in general support, usually positioned in field exercises and maneuvers near the center of the Division sector and in rear of the other artillery battalions. There was also the 81st Engineer Battalion, the 331st Medical Battalion and numerous special troops assigned to Division Headquarters, with their commanders on Division Staff.

The summer and early autumn of 1943 were devoted to basic artillery training, not only of the recruits, but of the young officers and noncommissioned officers. This period of about six months was also very productive in developing the skills of unit commanders and staff, in correlating the operations of the various units within the three combat commands, and within the Division as a whole, giving every promise of its becoming an effective, composite fighting force.

Three of the artillery battalion commanders were graduates of the Academy at West Point, promoted rapidly from lieutenants to lieutenant colonels since Pearl Harbor. It began to appear as the summer wore on (and wore out many peace time regular army officers who had never worked 12 to 15 hour days) that two of these West Pointers were letting their units fall behind in performance and responsiveness. The 591st failed in early tests; the 589th not only failed tests, but its commander was frequently difficult to find.

I do not know who made the decision (it was probably a consensus) but in late summer the Division Artillery Commander and the nonproductive commanders of the two artillery battalions were "reclassified" (reassigned to positions for which they were deemed to be better qualified). As I had felt when I was on the staff of the 1st Battalion of the 116th Field Artillery Regiment and a vacancy had occurred in the command of Battery B, I suddenly felt a compulsion to ask for a transfer to command of the 589th, the worst artillery battalion in the division, and perhaps in the whole army. Colonel Craig, with whom I now saw eye to eye on many aspects of our service, promised to discuss my reassignment with the new Division Artillery Commander, Brigadier General Leo T. McMahon. Apparently, the Colonel was as persuasive as usual; within days I received an order, signed by General McMahon, transferring me to the 589th, as its commander. Perhaps I would not have been so eager or so complacent if I had been able to visualize all of the catastrophic events that were to befall that (now my) battalion.

I was convinced that drastic measures were necessary if the 589th was to be made ready to support the 422nd in combat within a year. I called a meeting of all officers of the battalion at 1900 hours on the night following my appointment. The meeting was to be held in the large room at battalion headquarters where I was waiting following the evening meal, but at 1900 only slightly more than half of the complement of officers had arrived. When the last to appear straggled in at about 1920, I opened the meeting with an announcement that such lax discipline would no longer be tolerated and that anyone who was late for any scheduled event would be confined to the Post for one week. This was very drastic punishment, particularly for the married officers who lived with their families off Post, as did I.

Within the following week I received reports of three or four junior officers who were late for a drill or a meeting, and all of them received orders not to leave Fort Jackson for a full seven days. Although I demanded that the respective battery commanders report any violation of these orders, none was received. I began to notice a difference in the demeanor of the officers of the battalion, and even of the enlisted men. But the best of intentions and the fairest of orders can sometimes backfire.

A week or so later the Division went into a remote area of the range for a 3-day field exercise. When I received notice of a meeting of battalion commanders at Division Artillery Headquarters at 1500 hours on the second day, I made a mental note of the time but was not sure of the location of the Headquarters. At about 1430 I had my driver call for instructions on how to reach the Headquarters and he announced that it was located many miles away over unimproved wooded trails. Despite breaking all records for speed through a forest, I was 6 minutes late in arriving at the meeting. For one week I slept in the barracks with my men, and Jean brought a cocktail to the Post at 1800 each day, which we shared in a quiet spot near battalion headquarters. Strangely enough, this self-imposed disciplinary action (when no one else in the battalion knew I was late for a meeting except my faithful driver) did more to unite the men under my command than any measure I adopted for that purpose.

By October, 1943, the Division was deemed ready to demonstrate its prowess in field maneuvers under simulated battlefield conditions. Each of the maneuvers was planned, attended and critiqued by representatives of Army Ground Forces, and pitted against each other "Red" and "Blue" forces consisting of several divisions, corps artillery, engineers and even Air Corps units. Most of our fire missions were simulated (to limit casualties) but umpires checked our fire data and even the settings on our howitzers to determine and grade the effectiveness of our plotted concentrations (areas of impact of battalion volleys of projectiles).

The Division maneuvered for approximately four months, with periods of rest, reorganization, planning and preparation between maneuvers. The first area visited was in Chester and York Counties in north central South Carolina, between the towns of Chester and Rock Hill. I am sure that the infusion of tens of thousands of soldiers, the congestion on the roads and highways, the broken fences and the bivouacs in the fields, the constant noise of engines and movement, in the air and on the ground, were most unwelcome to the residents (although the area was undoubtedly selected because of its sparse population). But the adverse reaction was well restrained by the residents whom I contacted, possibly due to fringe benefits such as accrued to "Aunt Maggie", from whom Jean rented a room in Rock Hill for the duration.

Our Division received what we considered to be favorable ratings in the South Carolina maneuvers. After a brief period for refitting and replacement of vacancies we went over-the-road to north central Tennessee for more of the same. The maneuver area was in Rutherford and Wilson Counties, between Lebanon and Murfreesboro. A large number of divisions were involved in rugged country and miserable weather throughout the balance of the winter; we were beginning at last to apprehend what war was like.

My brother, Captain Marsden G. Kelly, had completed basic pilot training in Texas, and had been assigned as a B-24 pilot. By a most fortuitous circumstance, he was assigned to a B-24 pilot's school at an airfield near Murfreesboro while I was in the

23

area. I managed to break away for an afternoon between maneuvers and accompany him on a training mission. He was in the front seat of the cabin on the port side, the captain instructing him was beside him on the starboard side, I was behind the captain and there were two or three others seated in the cabin.

The instructor, who also had a set of controls, would do certain things to the aircraft and tell my brother to correct them. I was amazed when the instructor shut off one of the outboard engines and told my brother to turn in the opposite direction, away from the dead engine. It took all of my brother's strength, and perspiration was pouring down his face and neck (although the temperature in the cabin was in the 30's) when he completed the turn. I was told that the controls on the B-24, while assisted to some extent by pulleys, were hand operated, not mechanized. And then something happened to make me a believer.

When all of the training exercises had been completed and we were returning to base, the captain asked if I would like to take the controls. Although I had never been in the pilot's seat of any plane on take-off or landing, I had piloted in flight the little Piper L-4's that were used in the artillery for observed fire. I readily agreed to change places with my brother. But I was not prepared for the instructor to shut off the port, outboard engine and direct me to turn to starboard. I struggled with hands and feet and the perspiration began to flow, but all I was able to do was hold the plane level and fly straight ahead. I was about to order the captain to cut out the foolishness when suddenly he shut off the port, inboard engine and told me to hold the plane steady on course. Although I used all the strength at my command, we gradually went into a spin to port and started a sharp descent. The instructor roared with laughter (after all he had humiliated a lieutenant colonel without fear of retribution), took over the controls and brought the port engines on line. By the time we reached ground, I was able to thank him for the experience. But I didn't ask to go on any more training flights with my brother.

Before the completion of the Tennessee maneuvers, I was temporarily assigned as commander of a group of four battalions of corps artillery (an assignment that, if permanent, generally merits the rank of "full" or "bird" colonel). I wasn't sure I knew what to do with more than one battalion of artillery and was as apprehensive as I had been when the B-24 went into a spin. But I found that handling corps artillery was relatively easy; battalions don't require as much movement as organic artillery, they are farther to the rear and have more room to maneuver, and they don't have to take orders from the infantry. But still I was glad to get back to my regular job.

During our last maneuver in Tennessee, I was informed by Colonel Craig that we were going to Camp Atterbury, Indiana for testing and final training and refitting for combat. Atterbury was located in the southern, central area of the state, primarily in Johnson County, between Franklin and Columbus. Believing that we had only two or three more months to be together, Jean left our two children with her parents and found us a room in Franklin while the Division again moved over-the-road to Atterbury. We arrived at the end of March, in a blizzard that left four inches of snow on the ground.

When we were still at Fort Jackson, all units of the Division had lost seasoned and trained troops as replacements for other divisions that were scheduled to go overseas before we were. But when we arrived at Atterbury, we hoped, and had every reason to believe, that we would be permitted to take overseas the units we had devoted a year to training. The week after we arrived we learned that this was not to be. During April the Division lost 3,600 men (800 of them artillerymen in the lower grades) to replacement centers. The soldiers sent to us as replacements were primarily raw recruits, but to our dismay many of them were rejects from other units which had embarked and were on their way to Europe and the Pacific. In most cases, we were able to discern early on why they had been rejected by their units.

None of the unit commanders in the Division appreciated losing soldiers who had been tested and who had proven their worth in maneuvers, or receiving as substitutes the misfits of other outfits whom our men had replaced. And this was particularly true of the artillery units who were facing the Army Ground Forces (AGP) tests soon to be held at Camp Atterbury. These were intended as a means of ascertaining whether or not an artillery battalion was ready for combat and consisted of three exercises. The first was the rapid occupation of positions by the three firing batteries and parts of Headquarters Battery and firing on targets of opportunity (observed fire adjusted by the battery commander or FO's). The second was a daylight occupation of positions with a survey of the target area, and firing battalion concentrations on targets located by survey and on targets of opportunity. The third was a daylight reconnaissance and survey, nighttime occupation of positions and firing battalion concentrations on surveyed targets, and daylight (dawn) forward displacement.

The tests were observed and graded by artillery officers assigned by a higher headquarters, and were designed to determine the proficiency and combat readiness of the battalion in every aspect of its required performance. Of course, I participated in the testing of the 589th and could not observe all phases of the exercises, but we seemed to accomplish our missions and I was well pleased with our overall performance. I later learned (from Colonel Craig) that we had graded out slightly better than any other battalion of artillery in the Division. Had the worst battalion of artillery in the 106th become the best? I thought so.

CHAPTER V

My Longest Ten Minutes

Thomas P. Kelly, Jr.

In early summer we were momentarily expecting our order for overseas duty, and indeed we deemed ourselves ready despite the raid on our personnel. The news that a high level entourage from Washington, led by Under Secretary of War Patterson, was to visit the Division did nothing to diminish our satisfaction with our progress or our expectations. A few days before this distinguished group's arrival, Colonel Craig advised me that General Jones had decided to put on a show for the Under Secretary and John McCloy, who also would be among our prestigious guests, and that it had been decided to employ a combat team in a simulated advance into enemy territory, accompanied by the massed fire of an artillery battalion simulating a creeping barrage (one that moves forward in successive volleys just ahead of advancing troops). The 589th was the battalion selected for the demonstration. So somebody else thought we were the best artillery battalion in the Division, and he was almost proved to be wrong.

I was given explicit instructions. As battalion commander, I was to occupy a high point near the viewing stand (a platform filled with chairs where the visiting contingent and the Division Commander and General Staff were to sit). I would be accompanied by my battery commanders and members of my staff and would deliver my "battalion order" into a telephone wired to a loud speaker at the viewing stand. This order was prescribed by regulations and informed all units of the battalion of the positions they were to occupy (as they would be led to them by guides), registration [2] by one of the firing batteries (usually Battery B in the center) and all the other information they needed to go into action in support of the regiment (three battalions and special troops) of infantry. Of course, the entire procedure would be shortened for demonstration purposes; my firing batteries would already be in their positions when the order was given.

The attention of the viewers would then be directed to the combat infantry in a line about 1,000 yards in front of the viewing stand. It would be explained that the line of infantrymen were to begin their advance at 1400 hours and that they were to be in spread formation and advance by short bursts of running for intervals not exceeding about 5 seconds, before falling to the ground behind such cover as they could find. Before the advance of the infantry, my Battery B would register on the battalion aiming point (AP) and fire direction center would then take over and give

---

[2] This is accomplished by adjusting fire (by observing the bursting of projectiles) on a terrain feature (base point) located on the units' maps and recording the base deflection, or deviation from grid north (true north). The artillery weapons (pieces) are then laid on targets by a measured deviation from base deflection and to a measured or observed range (distance).

firing data to each howitzer battery. At my command the three batteries were to fire one volley of air bursts 500 yards ahead of the infantry as the latter began their advance to simulate a creeping barrage (air bursts are much more effective against troops in the open than percussion or graze bursts and are achieved by using time fuses, that burst the projectiles 20-30 yards above ground, rather than percussion fuses that burst the projectiles on impact). The volley, when fired at the demonstration, would go over an area well to the left of the viewing stand, but would go directly over the advancing troops, most of whom had never heard the railroad-train-like roar of twelve 4+ inch diameter projectiles traveling near the speed of sound just overhead.

The day of the demonstration arrived and I was convinced that we were ready. The entire battalion had put on a dress rehearsal (except the use of live ammunition) on the day before without a hitch. I was crouched and waiting on my OP with my complement of officers when the viewers, numbering about one hundred in numerous vehicles and including the distinguished officials from Washington, turned off of the main north-south road of the Post into a side road to our left leading to the viewing stand. The last vehicle cleared the intersection just before 1330, when I was supposed to deliver my battalion order, but I waited until they were settled in their seats. I thought the order was flawlessly delivered and after withdrawing from the OP I proceeded to my phone just in rear of the viewing stand where I was to give my FDC the order to fire the volley.

As I reached my station, there was a sharp but heavy explosion at the very intersection that the last vehicle had cleared only minutes earlier. I looked at the viewers, who had all turned toward the point of the explosion, but apparently they decided that the explosion was just a part of the show and turned their attention back to the speaker who was describing the exercise. I knew that Battery B's Captain Arthur C. Brown was just beginning to register the Battery on the AP and that the intersection where the explosion occurred was immediately under the gun-target (GT) line. I grabbed my phone and rang fire direction.

"What in the hell happened?", I asked.

"Captain Brown reported a short on the first round of registration", was the reply. (A "short" is any round that is fired at a range substantially less than that intended and ordered). The registration was continuing, but very slowly, and I asked why. I was told that Captain Brown had ordered 1st Lieutenant Kiendl, his Executive Officer, personally to check the range setting before each round was fired. And then Major Elliott Goldstein, who was in command at the fire direction center, came to the phone and said, "And I am going to have all of the battery executives check the range settings on all of the pieces before our concentration is fired unless you order me not to."

I said nothing, but my mind was rapidly weighing the pros and cons. It was 1355 and Battery B was just completing registration. It would require at least five minutes for the fire direction center to compute and transmit to the firing batteries the data for firing the volley, which was to be fired at 1400. And it would

32

take at least that long for each of the three battery executives to check the ranges on four howitzers. So we would be late in delivering our concentration. Should I tell the infantry commander to hold his troops until we were ready? That would admit failure and misplaced confidence. Should I tell Goldstein not to have the executives check the range settings? What if there was another short and some soldiers were killed? Unthinkable.

"Proceed with your plan, but tell the executives to run from piece to piece", I said and hung up.

I looked at my watch. It was 1400. I thought that the infantry might wait for our volley to jump off. But no, hundreds of soldiers sprang from the ground and ran 10 to 15 yards and dropped to the ground again. How many yards would they cover in a minute? In five minutes? Should I order a cease fire and ruin the whole demonstration? The soldiers were moving again. I looked at the phone and thought the most fervent prayer I have ever offered.

"God, let it ring, make it ring!"

I looked at my watch; it was 1405. The infantry were still moving forward; they must have traveled 200 of the 500 yards separating their starting point from the area of the air volley. But if I gave an order to increase the range by 200 yards, it would require another five minutes for all the battery executives to make another check of the range setting on each piece. I reached for the phone and it rang. I heard the most welcome and wonderful sentence I had ever heard,

"Battalion ready to fire", the operator said.

"Fire!", I said with alacrity, with all of the breath left in my body.

In seconds, I heard the sound of twelve pieces, firing as one, and then heard the "whirring" noise of flying projectiles at a distance. I looked at the target area and all advancing infantry had heard the same sounds and were prone. Then there was the sight of 11 simultaneous red flashes 20 to 25 yards above the ground and one very near the surface, all in an area of about 150 square feet some 200-300 yards beyond the line of infantry. I couldn't speak, but I certainly could think another prayer, this time of fervent thanks.

When later I was asked by several people in the know why I had withheld firing the volley for five extra minutes, I said simply,

"Well, it made things more realistic, didn't it?"

The answer was invariably, "Yes, it sure did."

I even received a special commendation of my Battalion's performance from General Jones. I believe that to this day nobody except Battery B and the Fire Direction Center knows there was a short. I've never denied it, but I am glad no one has ever asked.

CHAPTER VI

Men Making the Difference

Thomas P. Kelly, Jr.

Whether any organization, and indeed any endeavor, is a success or failure usually depends upon the quality of the personnel involved. After I had been the Commander of the 589th for one year, I was able to make an accurate evaluation of all of the officers in the Battalion and most of the enlisted men. I knew then, and still believe, that we had far more than our share of outstanding performers who put the unit and their contribution to its success ahead of all other aspects of their lives.

Esprit is the essential element of success in all military units (and in most other areas of human endeavor) and it begins in the squads (in artillery, the sections). The 589th had from the beginning a strong core of section chiefs and other non-commissioned officers, with intense loyalty to the Battalion. Despite the raids on our enlisted men, including a few sergeants, we were able to maintain this backlog of esprit throughout the five batteries of the Battalion. If a battery commander found a weak link, he could evoke and expect immediate corrective action by the Battalion Commander. Personal loyalties or friendships cannot be a consideration when the esprit or performance of the unit is at stake.

Of course, for the non-commissioned officers to create and strengthen esprit in those under their command, they must first develop it within themselves, and this can be accomplished only if they have respect for their officers. The 589th was fortunate in having a group of exceptional officers below field grade, including 1st Lieutenant and Battery Executive Officers Wood, Kiendl and Wright (Batteries A, B and C in that order), Hockstad in Headquarters Battery and Leach in Service Battery (as the reader will discover when the going gets rough).

And the five battery commanders, Captains Mencke, Brown, Rockwell, Beans and Cagle (Batteries A, B, C, Headquarters and Service, in that order) were truly outstanding. It is a vast relief to any commander to know that, not only his unit commanders, but their units, will always be where they are supposed to be and ready to accomplish or to exceed the accomplishment of their missions.

The officers on Battalion Staff upon whom I relied the most were the two Majors, Parker and Goldstein, Captains Huxel and Tietze (who was sacrificed by me so he could become S-3 of the 590th) and 1st Lieutenant Cocke. The latter was S-2, Tietze was Survey Officer and Huxel was Assistant S-3. The two majors had exceptional qualifications. Parker was senior and, consequently, was originally assigned as Battalion Executive, but he had a degree and career in engineering, could use a slide rule and compass with more facility than Goldstein and I could use a knife and fork, and was a natural for S-3. As a lawyer, Goldstein had considerably more presence, was much

36

more authoritarian and was more sound and rapid in reaching judgments; all qualities of a commander (executive). So I switched their positions, and not only did the Battalion staff operate more smoothly, but each of the majors was happier and, much more importantly, was more efficient in the discharge of his duties (it is much easier and rewarding to fit the man to the job than to fit the job to the man).

I should like to believe that I was partially responsible for the substantial improvement in esprit and efficiency of the 589th, but my contribution, if any, was incidental. I did give the Battalion a fresh start in 1942, with emphasis on the concept that duty comes first, ahead of all other considerations. If this was helpful and productive of good results, I am satisfied.

C H A P T E R VII

The Time Has Come

Thomas P. Kelly, Jr.

When we first arrived at Atterbury, we were expecting to immediately receive an overseas departure date, but we were informed that we would have about three months' notice of our movement to a port of embarkation. So Jean again got busy in her secondary capacity as real estate bird dog and located a beautiful and spacious home for rent in Nashville, Indiana. This was (and I am sure is still) a very quiet and picturesque village about 20 miles south of the Camp, and before many weeks, several other officers had also located their families there, including Colonel Craig and Lieutenant Colonel Benjamin Hagman, my replacement as S-3 of Division Artillery (and also the former husband of Mary Martin, the universally known vocalist and actress, and the father by that marriage of Larry Hagman, destined for stardom on television, who lived with his father and the latter's new wife in Nashville). We three officers took turns driving the others to the Camp each morning for 6:30 a.m. reveille and home again at 9:30 p.m. after classes and a 15 hour day.

We received the first alert for embarkation in June, the second in July and specific orders (but secret, i.e., known only to senior officers) in August for movement to a staging area on the east coast, Camp

39

Miles Standish at Taunton, Massachusetts. We believed at that time (and had every reason to believe) that we would be permitted to take into combat the men whom we had worked so hard to train during the past spring and summer. But to our amazement, there was another raid on our junior officers (lieutenants) and men for replacements in Europe. All of those selected were audibly disgruntled (I would like to believe this was due to devotion to the 589th, and not to the prospect of early combat) until I assembled them at the time of their departure and told them that we disliked losing them more than they disliked leaving, but that we, and their replacements, would probably see combat before they did. In many instances, I am sure that this was true.

There were many trains, and there would be several ships, assigned to transport the division to the staging area and overseas; the 589th did not leave Atterbury until October 9. The cars were typical troop train cars with stacked bunks and no amenities. The two meals a day were K rations (cold boxed food with long shelf life) eaten in our seats due to the economy of space in the cars. Knowing there would be many more trying days in the near future, none of us minded the minor tribulations of the journey until the evening of October 10, when we stopped briefly in the station at Providence, Rhode Island. On the adjoining track was a passenger train of conventional design and the car on our troop train that I was in was opposite one of the luxurious dining cars typical of Pullman trains of the prewar era, with heavy linen table cloths and napkins and sparkling silverware. All of the seats were

40

occupied, about one fourth of them by American soldiers and the remaining three fourths by German officers, in their resplendent dress uniforms.

I was unbelieving, as were Majors Goldstein and Carter, and I sent a soldier to inquire about the identity of the German officers enjoying their evening repast in the dining car on the siding next to our troop train. We were informed by him that they were prisoners on their way to a prison camp in the midwest. We wondered why the army had bothered to have guards seated among them; obviously, they had never had it so good, and were not candidates for escape. I would remember this scene vividly two and a half months later when I was a passenger in a German prisoner train and my hosts did not miss a single opportunity to make my journey, and that of the one hundred other occupants of my cattle car, miserable and life threatening, as we shall see.

Taunton, even in October and before the onset of winter, was consistently dreary and the gloom was not wholly dissipated by an occasional trip to Boston, although the Commons and the surrounding theaters and restaurants offered attractive inducements. Again, contrary to our expectations, we were in Miles Standish for a full month, during which I prepared a Standard Operating Procedure (SOP) for a division 105 mm. artillery battalion, mostly for my own satisfaction, but avidly read and considered very helpful by many of the junior officers. I do not believe that a single copy survived the ensuing two months.

Without equipment of any kind, training was difficult and consisted of classes held by the batteries in barracks for the new replacements dealing primarily with discipline. We were all happy to finally receive orders to move to the Port of Boston on November 10, where we embarked upon the S.S. *Manhattan,* now refitted as a troop transport and renamed the USCGSS *Wakefield.* We were to make the trip to Liverpool, England, without a convoy or escort due to detection devices and the speed of which the vessel was capable. To my knowledge, no enemy submarine was sighted during our voyage.

One reason for our unimpeded and unmolested trip to England was the weather in the north Atlantic during November. Despite the constant wind of near gale strength, visibility was limited to a few hundred yards by mist and rain. The latter required troops to remain in their sleeping quarters where their bunks were stacked four or five deep and there was little room to move around. Due to the rolling and pitching of the *Wakefield,* most meals found a final resting place on the bunks or the deck, and there was a constant series of clean up crews in action (these required frequent changes because of the effect of their work upon their own good health). After two or three trips to the hold where most of the men were quartered, I deemed it wise to spend time in my own relatively comfortable quarters or on deck, despite the rain and the fog. We arrived at Liverpool by way of St. Georges Channel on November 17, and proceeded to Gloucester by train.

Gloucester was typical of all industrial cities that had been living under the demands and restrictions of war for a period of more than five years. Blacked out at night and very active during daylight hours, all industry was directed to the war effort. This means that 90% of the population was, willingly or unwillingly, producing materials and sons for the armed forces or other war-related goals. The other 10% seemed to be living off the thousands of American soldiers billeted there waiting for transport to the continent. These ranged from bartenders to prostitutes to jewelry peddlers on street corners. Of course, they may have considered that even their services contributed to the war effort; the front had many facets and many diversions.

We were issued new vehicles and other equipment required by our Table of Organization (TO), but training was limited to classes, mainly on German recognition and German tactics. On December 1, we proceeded south in column in our new vehicles, fully equipped except for ammunition. We camped at Waymouth that night and boarded two Landing Ships Tank (LST's) the next morning in Portland Harbor. On December 3, we made a very rough crossing of the English Channel and anchored off the coast of France, barely within binocular range of LeHavre and the mouth of the Seine River. So far our surroundings were more akin to a paid vacation than to the bloodiest war in history.

On the next day, we had to wait our turn to enter the Seine, which was jammed with vessels of all types, mostly American. We started up river that afternoon, anchored in darkness that night and arrived at Rouen at noon on December 5. During that morning, we witnessed many signs of the devastation of war, set incongruously against a background of the beautiful French countryside. Blackened tanks and artillery pieces with broken carriages abandoned by the Germans in their hasty and largely disorganized retreat from Caen and the Falaise pocket. We saw the same signs of warfare, together with bomb craters, shell-racked houses, buildings and bridges along the way, when we left Rouen in our own vehicles on December 7, in column with the 422nd. We wondered if the French would ever be motivated to restore the orderly beauty of their countryside, villages and towns. Perhaps they half expected a turn around in the fortunes of war, and another German invasion.

We traveled the "Red Ball Express"[3] to our encampment near the Belgian city of Roselle that night. It was difficult for me to believe that I had been in the Army for more than four years and America had been engaged in global warfare for three years, and I still had not seen or heard a shot fired in anger. But that was soon to change.

All regimental and Battalion Commanders met with General Jones and his staff at a beautiful manor house where he had established his Command Post (CP). We were to proceed on the next day to St. Vith, Belgium, near the German border, where Division would establish its permanent headquarters. We were to replace "man for man and gun for gun" the 2nd Infantry Division, which was in position on and west

---

[3] A highway route for supplies established by the Americans across France and Belgium to the front in Germany, and connecting with roads serving the ports of debarkation.

of the Schnee Eifel (a ridge rising out of the Ardennes plain about twenty-five miles in length extending generally east and then north from a point west of Bleialf to Roth in extreme West Germany). Until captured by the Americans in November, the Schnee Eifel had been an important segment of the Siegfried Line and the commanders of various infantry units of the 2nd Division were enjoying occupancy of the German bunkers as their respective headquarters.

Upon our arrival in St. Vith on December 8, the 589th was assigned a bivouac area on the St. Vith-Schönberg road and I was summoned to Division Headquarters to receive orders for the occupation of our positions. All of the commanders of regiments, battalions and special troops were addressed by General Jones, who announced that the elements of the Division would begin to occupy the positions then held by the 2nd Division on the night of December 9-10 in blackout conditions and with minimum sound in order to prevent the enemy from learning that the 2nd Division was being withdrawn. That Division was moving north to participate in a "top secret" attack scheduled for a few days later to prevent the destruction of the Roer River dams by the retreating German forces, with consequent flooding of the American route of advance.

I was told that my Battalion had the honor of being the first unit of the Division to occupy its position in order that we could register on the Division Artillery Base Point (base point) for the benefit of all of the artillery battalions in the Division. The 2nd Division was to start its withdrawal that night and my Fire

Direction Center and one of my firing battery sections were to occupy positions after 1600 hours on December 9 and register on the base point before dark. All commanders were to reconnoiter their units positions after 1600 on December 9, and establish liaison with their counterparts in the 2nd Division for briefing.

On the following morning, I had no difficulty finding the CP of my corresponding battalion of the 2nd Division. It was located approximately two-thirds of the way from Bleialf to Auw on the road connecting those two towns (see map on appendix i for locations of the CP's of the 589th, the 422nd and the 423rd, and the positions of my firing batteries). My counterpart commander was busy with his battalion's displacement, and I was briefed by his Executive Officer, a Major with many months of combat experience. Over a cup of coffee in his Headquarters Battery's Mess, he tried to acquaint and impress me with the inherent dangers of our position. He pointed out that the Division's sector had a front of 28 miles, four or five times the length of the normal front for a division in a defense posture. Further, our batteries would be exposed to an enemy advancing from the east with nothing in front of us except a reinforced squadron of cavalry (light tanks and armored cars). He demonstrated by reference to my map that substantially all of the Division's infantry positions were south and west of our batteries and could not protect us from, or come to our rescue in the event of, a sudden attack from the east or northeast through the open plain north of Auw-Rath (known as the "Losheim Gap").

I listened patiently to the Major (the coffee was welcome after our ride in -20° weather), [4] but I was not impressed with his warning of danger. After all, did we not have the Germans on the run, and didn't they have more than they could handle on their eastern front? I attributed the Major's polemic to an attempt to justify the assignment of the great 2nd Division to a "quiet sector" of the front. But I would remember his words with considerably more respect eight days later.

I reconnoitered all of the gun positions with the Major and went up on the Schnee Eifel with him for designation of the Division Artillery Base Point. I then returned to the bivouac area with high expectations of firing our first rounds in anger. I explained to the assembled officers of the Battalion how to reach their respective positions, marking them on their maps for night occupations, and emphasized the order that no gun position could be altered in any respect. I then led the fire direction section and one gun section from A Battery into their positions and registration was duly accomplished by A Battery's forward observer (FO). The 106th Division was in the War.

Throughout the week of December 9 to 15, the 106th Division was indeed in a quiet sector. There was

---

[4] The ambient temperature varied between -10°F. and -30°F. throughout the winter months, and, consequently, prevailed during the entire period covered by this narrative. There was a slight amelioration in early April, 1945.

a minimum of firing on targets of opportunity and for interdiction east and south of the Schnee Eifel. The weather remained cold and overcast, with a ceiling of 500 to 1,000 feet, and the ground had a snow cover of one to two feet. We saw no aircraft of any description or allegiance, but there was a VI launching site near Prum (southeast of the Schnee Eifel) and "buzz bombs" were constantly flying overhead at a height of approximately 500 feet directed at targets in Belgium and perhaps England, although we had several "shorts" that fell and exploded just beyond our positions.

With limited firing through our fire direction center, I took advantage of many opportunities to visit Headquarters of the 422nd and its front lines, and became very familiar with the disposition of its forces and the terrain. Due to the escarpment that formed the south slope of the Schnee Eifel, the infantry's position along its crest was virtually impenetrable to frontal attack. But the last (north) outpost of the Division was southeast of Roth and the southernmost strong point of the next infantry division in the line (the 99th) was several miles to the north. While I did not (and do not) consider myself an infantry tactician, I wondered by whose design so much confidence and responsibility was being placed in a few hundred cavalrymen in the gap.

When I put this question to my Combat Team Commander, whom by now I addressed by his nickname "Desch", he just shrugged his shoulders. "They won't let us do anything about it," he said. The Roer Dam operation had not yet jumped off and VIII

Corps insisted that there would be no change in disposition of the Division's forces.

Arthur C. Brown

From December 7th to 15th we proceeded to dig and settle into fixed positions. Our infantry occupied a segment of the German Siegfried line. As this fortification naturally faced away from Germany, our troops had to face the wrong way to defend against an attack from the east or southeast. As the 589th Field Artillery was on the extreme left, with only a cavalry screen protecting our left flank, our outfit was extremely vulnerable. Our front was Hitler's choice and Eisenhower's "calculated risk". We were untried troops, with no combat experience, and in an impossible defensive position. We had replaced an artillery battalion of the 2nd Infantry Division; and while the relieved troops took their home-made stoves out of the dugouts and carried them to their new positions, we were indebted to the men of the 2nd for some tips they gave us on how to run a war. As an example, these veterans told us that you had to split your eight-man gun crew into two parts. This maneuver allowed half the men to rest while the other half manned the guns, thus permitting continuous service of the pieces twenty-four hours a day. In training the situation of continuous action never occurred, and the training manuals did not mention this technique. The manuals were probably written by people who also had no combat experience.

John R. Schaffner

The 106th Infantry Division relieved the 2nd Infantry Division, and we took over the positions of the 15th Field Artillery Battalion. They were in position about one and a half miles southeast of Auw, Germany. The battalion command post was set up in the kitchen of a substantial German house just to the rear of the firing batteries. These batteries took over the dugouts and log huts vacated by the men of the 15th Field Artillery Battalion. The howitzers were put into the same emplacements dug by the 15th, and in some cases the guns were simply swapped, since it was easier than trying to extricate the pieces already in place. A Battery was positioned on the south side of the road to Auw, and B and C Batteries on the north side. There was much snow, and the drivers had big problems once they left the hard roads. The snow made it almost impossible to move off the roads, which later had the effect of channeling the German attack down the hard road. Service Battery was sent into position a few miles to the rear, about four miles south of Schönberg, Belgium. We were told by the 15th Field Artillery men that we had come into a very quiet sector where nothing ever happened. They weren't happy about leaving, and when we saw what relatively comfortable quarters they were vacating we didn't blame them. I shared a dugout that was roofed over with heavy logs and had a jerry-can stove, just like uptown. We had been able to register A Battery, and the battalion was able to commence fire on December 9. We were feeling rather secure since, after

50

all, our infantry was supposed to be between us and the Germans. It sounded good to me. We were supporting the 422nd Infantry Regiment, which was occupying the first belt of pillboxes of the Siegfried line, which had been breached at this point the previous October.

Our guns were usually firing during the night, but since visibility was poor, it was unobserved. Headquarters Battery crews reported being fired upon, and on one occasion an enemy plane circled the area for an hour or more. Numerous flares were seen on the north flank of the battalion, and one night an enemy patrol was reported to be in the area. During this period most of my time was spent at various outposts near the battery position. There was nothing to report. (As to those facts of which I had no knowledge, I relied upon Francis R. Aspinwall's "History of the 589th Field Artillery Battalion," published on pp. 81-89 of *The Cub of the Golden Lion – Passes in Review* hereafter referred to as "Aspinwall".)

Elliott Goldetein

Not only were the gun crews divided into a day and night shift, the entire battalion operated on that basis. As battalion executive, I worked the night shift and was in command during the night hours, and Lieutenant Colonel Thomas P. Kelly Jr., battalion commander, was in command during the day. The other headquarters officers were Major Arthur C. Parker, battalion S-3, Captain George Huxel, assistant S-3, and First Lieutenant Joseph Cocke, S-2. Major Parker, a graduate engineer, and a reserve officer who

51

had served on active duty for several years in the early thirties, was better qualified to run the fire direction center than I, so I was made battalion executive even though I was junior to Major Parker. Each of the staff positions of the battalion headquarters was divided between day and night shifts. Personnel of a field artillery battalion in a fixed combat position were on duty in the same pattern as workers in a manufacturing plant on 12-hour shifts, one-half of the artillery personnel working each shift. Everyone had adjusted to his shift, the battalion had shaken down, and we felt quite confident that we were able to perform our duties in support of the 422nd Infantry.

During our settling-in period, I reconnoitered the area and met a cavalry officer, Lieutenant DeJongh Franklin, an old friend from Atlanta. He was on reconnaissance and approached me in a scout car. He warned me that his 14th Cavalry Group was attempting to cover nine miles of undefended front. His scout car was lightly armored, and in the event of attack, he could only report and run. So I was warned of our vulnerability.

On the night of the fifteenth I was on duty in the fire direction center at battalion headquarters, in command of the battalion. I commenced receiving reports from forward observers that major traffic was moving in the vicinity of Auw and convoys were seen moving with lights. Telephone wires connecting the battalion with forward observers assigned to infantry units were cut, flares were observed, and German patrols were reported in the area.

Intelligence should flow from the infantry regiments and field artillery battalions who are in contact with the enemy back to division (in our case through division artillery) and from there to Corps Headquarters and on to Army Headquarters. We found that any information we gave higher headquarters was considered to be worthless. We had been puzzled by the order that we take over in place from an artillery battalion of the 2nd Infantry Division. The explanation given us was that those in command did not want the Germans to know that we had relieved the veteran 2nd Division. But when we reported that German radio had broadcast to us on our arrival, welcoming us to the position, and identifying all of our units, our orders were not changed to authorize us to improve our positions.

I found out how little our intelligence meant to the various headquarters during the night of December 15-16, when I reported the various incidents observed by our personnel to the division artillery intelligence officer (S-2), a West Pointer. He told me that he had been reporting these actions to the Division G-2 who had reported them to the Corps G-2, but had been assured that this was merely a diversion put on by the Germans to fool us into thinking that they were making an attack through our positions. Our division artillery S-2 said, "I've told them that this is the route that the Germans took through Belgium in 1870 and have taken in every war since. It's in their tactics manual, and it is a training exercise for all German officers. I've told them that, and they don't believe me.

53

They are convinced that the attack is coming well to the north of us."

CHAPTER VIII

December 16, 1944

Thomas P. Kelly, Jr.

My CP and the Battalion Fire Direction Center were located in the home of a German family, who had moved into the basement of the house next door. Inasmuch as my predecessor Battalion Commander had slept in the best bed in the house, and taking seriously the Corps' order of "man for man", I slept in the same bed. At about 0600 hours on December 16, I was awakened by explosions in very close proximity to the house. There had been some interdiction fire on a crossroad near the CP during the preceding week, but this was different. Within two minutes I was in the Fire Direction Center and talking by radio to the FOs.

The FOs for A and B Batteries were on the Schnee Eifel near the Headquarters of the 1st and 2nd Battalions, respectively, of the 422nd. They had little to report except sporadic artillery fire along the ridge and word of mouth reports of a fire fight near Roth, north and somewhat east of their positions. However, at my suggestion, the FO for C Battery was not with the regiment's 3rd Battalion on the Schnee Eifel, but was in the area of Schlausenbach-Kobscheid south and west of Roth. He was a small but very wiry young 2nd Lieutenant of Russian descent named Fomenko who allegedly could converse in seven languages, and I had always hoped that he was more articulate in the other six. But on this morning, his message was loud and clear: he had heard constant heavy firing to his northeast in the vicinity of Roth and was on his way there to find out what was going on. I cautioned him not to get too close but to keep us informed.

I also called the firing batteries and ordered them to be prepared to fire to the east and as far north as Roth. This was not an easy directive to follow because their pieces were not only laid south to southeast but the trails (the counter-balancing frames on which the tubes and wheels were mounted and by which the howitzers were towed) were in deep pits. These had originally been dug by our counterpart battalion of the 2nd Division because, due to the height of the Schnee Eifel, it was necessary to resort to "high angle" fire in order to target enemy forces charging the ridge. It was a Herculean task to lift the howitzers out of their pits and site them in another direction, but it was accomplished, together with Fomenko's registration on a new base point, within an hour and a half.

By this time Fomenko was in a position to see German forces, including tanks, on the Roth-Auw road. However, because elements of the friendly battalion of cavalry were also in the area, we did not attempt to take the advancing Germans under fire. I did report their presence to Colonel Malin Craig, our Division Artillery Executive, who was with General Jones at Division Headquarters in St. Vith. He did not seem too perturbed but told me to keep him informed. I took no further action at that time except to request C Battery to send another FO to the area south of Auw. I did not know that the Battery Executive, a 1st

Lieutenant named Thomas Wright, would undertake this assignment, but apparently his Battery Commander, Captain Malcolm B. Rockwell, took over his duties as commander of the gun sections so that Wright, a vigorous young man who was tough of body and mind, could carry out this dangerous undertaking.

During the morning there was a feint by the enemy in front of the Schnee Eifel and we fired on a few targets of opportunity (which we were able to do without high angle fire). However, the situation worsened rapidly after noon. Fomenko and Wright reported enemy troops, vehicles and tanks entering Auw without opposition (I was later informed that the cavalry forces had withdrawn). I had earlier ordered Captain James B. Cagle, Jr., Commander of our Service Battery, in position west of the Schönberg-Bleialf road, to bring all available ammunition to the firing batteries. This had been accomplished and Captain Cagle reported that he was attempting to obtain more rounds from the Division ammunition dump. We opened fire on the Germans in Auw (except for C Battery due to a large stand of trees in its line of fire to the east), and reported the enemy's advance to Division Artillery Headquarters. Brigadier General Leo T. McMahon, the Division Artillery Commander, wanted numbers and when I reported to him that there was at least a battalion of infantry and a troop of tanks, as estimated by Fomenko, he was incredulous. He laughed and said my forward observer must have a flair for the dramatic. Apparently at this point Division G-2 considered the enemy activity to be a reconnaissance in force rather than an attack. I informed General McMahon that I had been to my battalion's outpost and, "It looks pretty damn serious to me."

During the early afternoon the situation deteriorated precipitously. My Headquarters Battery Commander, Captain Alva R. Beans, and his Executive Officer drove their jeep into the area east of B Battery and just north of the junction of the Bleialf-Auw road and the road to Schlausenbach, where they came under fire from German foot soldiers dressed in snow suits and completely invisible at a distance greater than 200 feet. Both of the Americans were hit before they could get away; Captain Beans was so seriously wounded that he was evacuated immediately. This incident put in train a number of events. I ordered B and C Batteries to send detachments with machine guns and carbines to dig in immediately in front of their gun positions to take under fire the snow-suited Germans. This was accomplished and after a few rounds were exchanged the Germans withdrew and began a flanking action around the north or rear of C Battery. This move was to lead to disaster, but for the moment we had respite from duty as foot soldiers (infantry), for which we were not fully prepared.

Despite the constant firing by two batteries into Auw, the Germans continued their advance westward down the Auw-Wischeld Road in rear of C Battery and in the direction of the 592nd Field Artillery Battalion, the Division's medium artillery (155 mm. howitzers), which was in position northwest of our positions and south of Andler. It was impossible for us to fire on this advance, but almost immediately we were confronted by a new target. A column of tanks left Auw on the Bleialf road headed for the heart of my Battalion. We immediately shifted our fire to this column as directed by Lieutenant Wright, who proved to be an excellent FO. After we had massed our fire for several rounds on the column, knocking out at least one tank, Lieutenant Wright sent fire direction this last message "Down 100 (range), right 100 (deflection), fire for effect, and give me 20 seconds to get the hell out of here or they will fall on me. " We waited the 20 seconds and after the order to fire was given we could hear the rounds exploding over his radio as though they had landed in the next room.

Most of the tanks then withdrew, but one continued on the road toward our Command Post and reached its junction with the Schlausenbach Road. At that point 1st Lieutenant Eric Wood, Executive of A Battery, took the lone tank under direct fire by his No. 1 section and knocked it out with the second or third round using armor piercing projectiles. It appeared for the moment that we had been saved from immediate invasion.

Of course, all of this was reported to Division Artillery Headquarters as it occurred, and gradually it appeared from the responses we received that Division and Corps were taking us seriously. We were told to hang on. But then there was the most serious development of a long day. For the last hour we had been having difficulty hearing our FOs due to interference by German transmissions on our frequency. This condition had worsened and by the middle of the afternoon our reception was limited to the guttural commands of the advancing enemy. When

I attempted to report this development to Division Artillery, I found that, probably due to the shelling of the Schonberg-Bleialf road by the Germans, we had lost communication by telephone. I gave an order to Headquarters Battery to trace and repair the line and damn the projectiles.

I knew by reports from C Battery that the Germans were attacking their gun position from the east and the north and had probably reached the town of Andler. Consequently, I was not surprised to see the entire 592nd Field Artillery Battalion emerging from the trail to our B and C Batteries and turn west on the Bleialf-Auw road. My immediate reaction was that the 592nd had received a displacement order from Division Artillery and we may have received one also if we had not lost communication. (I learned that night that Lieutenant Colonel Richard E. Weber, Jr., Commander of the 592nd, having been attacked and threatened with encirclement by the Germans and having lost his communication with Division Artillery, made the decision to evacuate; the Battalion continued its retreat and was west of St. Vith before it stopped to await orders. In my opinion, Weber made the correct decision.)

There was then a development that could have caused me to give a similar order. The tanks that had made the earlier move toward our position from Auw, and had paid the price, were light tanks. At about 1700 hours we received a message from our outpost, located beside the road to Auw and beyond a barn about 300 yards east of the CP, that a medium tank was approaching from the east with guns blazing. I called A Battery to order direct fire, but I had trouble getting through to the gun position, and as I finally did so, I looked up into the smiling face of my Executive Officer, Major Elliott Goldstein. It was the first smile I had seen that day. Major Goldstein casually informed me that he and an outpost guard had knocked out the tank with one round from the bazooka with which the guard was armed. There were no more tank attacks on our position.

John R. Schaffner

At 0605 in the morning, before dawn, our position was hit by a barrage of German artillery fire. I was on guard at one of our outposts, and though I did not realize it at the time, I was probably better off there than with the rest of the battery. We had a 50-caliber machine gun in a dug-in position, so being somewhat protected, I got down in the lowest possible place and "crawled into my helmet." During the shelling, many rounds exploded real close and showered dirt and tree limbs about us, but also there were quite a few duds that only smacked into the ground. Those were the "good" ones as far as I was concerned. After about thirty minutes, the shelling ceased, and before any of the enemy came into sight, I was summoned to return to the battery position. Aspinwall states that, from an inspection of the fragments, it was determined that the enemy was using 88-, 105-, and 155-millimeter guns.

Elliott Goldstein

As soon as I was relieved by Lieutenant Colonel Kelly on the morning of the sixteenth, I took a crew out with an aiming circle to make shell reports. The purpose of a shell report is to make it possible to locate the enemy artillery. The only equipment necessary is an aiming circle. The procedure is to set up the aiming circle pointed along the line of flight of the shell, which is easily determined by an inspection of the site of the explosion. The size of the crater indicates the caliber of the gun, and the direction from which it came is clearly indicated by the shape of the crater. The crater will also indicate the angle of the trajectory. By taking readings on a number of craters, it is possible to map the location of each gun. While we were leisurely engaged in this activity, we heard sounds which sounded like firecrackers popping in the distance. We looked up and saw our first German enemies on a slope to the right front, about one hundred yards away, dressed in white overgarments with white hoods. The white garments blended very well with the snow. They were firing at us. No one was hit, and we were more indignant than frightened. We fired back, they withdrew and we returned to the battalion command post.

The 589th Field Artillery Battalion had two air liaison airplanes (Piper Cubs) assigned to its Headquarters Battery. Their principal mission was to act as the eyes of the artillery, by flying reconnaissance missions, and by observing and adjusting the firing of the pieces. Lieutenant Earl A. Scott was one of the pilots. Each pilot flew with an observer, who carried out the missions of observation and fire adjustment while the pilot flew the plane. Lieutenant Graham Cassibry, a forward observer in A Battery, sometimes flew as an observer with Lieutenant Scott. Lieutenant Cassibry had received fifty hours of pilot training, but was not a licensed or qualified pilot. The planes arrived at St. Vith and occupied the air strip there previously occupied by the 2nd Division.

Earl A. Scott

I had been told that we were going into a quiet sector. I drove up to the battalion CP to report in. The weather was foul, and I didn't attempt an aerial reconnaissance. However, on this day, December 16, the quiet was broken by the sound of artillery shells fired at St. Vith and at the battalion's position. The air strip, which was a mile from St. Vith, was not shelled. Since the weather was foul, the other flight officer and I chose to ride a jeep to the battalion CP. We never got there. Lieutenant Cassibry intercepted us with a message from the air officer for us to return to the airstrip. He needed a plane up for observation, and gave me the assignment and designated Lieutenant Cassibry to be my observer. We returned to the airstrip and took off in my Piper L-4 airplane. Flying towards the battalion position, at about fifteen hundred feet altitude, we received machine gun fire. We saw tracer bullets, and heard the zip, zip of bullets just a few feet in front of the plane. What to do? The evasive action I'd been taught at Fort Sill, the field artillery school, was to execute a diving turn, and come out over trees or bare ground, and then to hedgehop out of danger. Pilots with the 2nd Division Artillery had told us that this maneuver was useless, since the Germans were on to it. They didn't tell us, however, what maneuver to use. I did some rather tricky flying at that point, and eventually got us out of danger. Neither of us was hit. Upon returning to the airstrip, we found that the rear section of the fuselage was riddled with bullet holes. What a birthday celebration! I turned twenty-six that day.

John R. Schaffner

At about 0800 the battery positions again came under heavy artillery fire, and again no casualties were reported. At about 0900 communication was again established with Division and with the 422nd Infantry Regiment. However, the lines were soon shot out again by the enemy artillery, and after 1300 the battalion was for all practical purposes isolated from its supported regiment. Captain Alva R. Beans, the Commander of Headquarters Battery and communications officer, and Lieutenant Hockstad, assistant communications officer, went forward to the infantry regimental command post after 0900, and while returning were fired upon by white-dressed and white-hooded Germans and Captain Beans was severely wounded. He was brought in and later evacuated. At 0915 a report was received of enemy patrols in Auw. Lieutenant Wright from C Battery went forward to a position commanding a view of Auw, and from there

64

directed fire on the town until he was pinned down by small arms fire. C Battery was unable to bring guns to bear directly on Auw due to a high mask of trees between it and the target. About 1030 a patrol was sent out as additional security to man defensive positions along the road from Auw. Since it was now apparent that the enemy held Auw, an attack from that direction was expected. This patrol soon reported small arms fire from the enemy infantry moving out of Auw. An observation post was set up in the attic of the house in which a part of Headquarters Battery was quartered.

At about 1500 three enemy tanks were seen coming along the road from Auw towards the battalion command post. At about four hundred yards range, the lead tank opened fire on one of our outposts, damaging three machine guns. Small arms fire was directed against the tank, but it just "buttoned up" and kept coming. When it came within range of our bazookas, they were fired, and one hit and immobilized the lead tank. It was immediately hit again by an A Battery 105 howitzer round and burst into flames. The enemy crew bailed out and were killed by small arms fire. The second and third tanks also took hits but were able to withdraw to defiladed positions. One of the tanks kept up harassing fire from a hull-down position, but counterfire was directed at it, and it is believed that it too was knocked out. The effective work of this patrol and our firing batteries kept the whole battalion position from being overrun that afternoon.

John F. Gatens

Some of the published accounts of the defense of the battalion positions by a howitzer from A Battery are actually incorrect. I know because I was the gunner serving under Sergeant Shook in the section which was in the number one position. Although we were then the number one section, we were in that position quite by accident. On the way to the assigned firing position, our truck broke down. The other three sections went on and we followed later. We entered the battalion area on a road going northeast to Auw, which passed through the middle of the battalion's position. A Battery's position was on the right of the road, and the other batteries were on the left. When we arrived, the howitzers which preceded us had occupied the two, three, and four positions, leaving the number one position open for us. Because of the snow it was difficult to maneuver into position, and if they had occupied the number one position, we would not have been able to go around them. The other positions were in defilade, the ground sloping up and then down from the road. My piece was on the high ground, and not masked by the higher ground in front of the others.

The battery was firing indirect fire when three tanks appeared, approaching on the Auw-Bleialf Road. Our gun was the only piece that could fire directly at the tanks, so we were obviously the section to fire on them. We were ordered to cease firing the missions given the battery, and to fire directly on the lead tank.

In direct fire with a 105-millimeter howitzer, the gunner is in charge. He must sight the piece in the

66

same way you aim a rifle but using a gunner's sight. The gunner's sight, which has vertical and horizontal crosshairs, and magnification, is mounted on the carriage to the left of the tube, and moves with the movement of the tube. Fortunately, we had been trained to do this, and I didn't hesitate. I aimed at the lead tank, by first setting the elevation to allow for my estimate of the distance to the tank, and then traversing the tube until I thought I had the howitzer aimed directly at the tank. I was looking through the sight and tracking the tank when four men came into view, racing toward us down the hill. I was afraid I might hit them if I fired at the tank, so my #1 cannoneer and I ran out in front of the gun, and by motioning with our arms that they should lie down, and yelling our brains out, we got the message to them. I was anxious that they lie down in place, instead of running toward us, since I didn't believe the tank had spotted us, and if they had continued towards us, they would have either been killed or attracted attention to our position.

As soon as I had a clear field of fire, I fired my first shot. The first round, fired on my command, missed the target. Sergeant Shook, who was standing behind me to observe through his binoculars, shouted, "It's a little high!" I lowered the elevation and gave the command to fire. It was a direct hit. We then fired another round for good measure. The tank blocked the road and prevented the other tanks from advancing. That was the first time the battalion engaged in direct fire--but it certainly wasn't the last.

After we completed firing on the tanks, I scanned the area but couldn't find the other tanks. We were then given a new fire mission. The elevation we received was the one and only time we were ordered to raise the tube to its maximum elevation. The command for the powder charge was either one or two powder bags. With the howitzer in its maximum elevation and a small powder charge, the shell will fly relatively high but will land a relatively short distance from the firing position. I believe we were firing on the other two tanks. To my knowledge, there was no other direct fire by the battery in that position.

I've often wondered, had the tanks not been stopped, whether we would have reached Baraque de Fraiture, or would we have been overrun and captured right there?

Charles F. Jacelon

I was assigned as forward observer sergeant in A Battery of the 589th. I served under Lieutenant Willard Crowley. Corporal Hugh Mayes was our radio operator and Private First Class Reed was the telephone operator. We had a comfortable cabin for six, and two of the infantrymen shared our quarters. Our observation post was on the forward slope of a hill in a tree line a few hundred yards from our quarters. Lieutenants Crowley and Reed were on the observation post from 0800 until noon, and Mayes and I manned the observation post from noon until 1600. For the five days that we occupied that position we saw no movement. On December 15 we were relieved by another forward observer team. The plan was that the several forward observer teams would rotate around several different positions to familiarize all the officers and their crews with our area of operations. Lieutenant Crowley's team was to spend the next period in the firing battery area with jeep servicing, laundry, baths, etc. We found unoccupied bunks in the hutments in the area and went to bed.

Before dawn on December 16 the battery area came under enemy artillery fire, and several V-1 buzz bombs flew over. A Battery started firing on orders from the fire direction center. Prum, Germany, was at the maximum range of our 105-mm. howitzers. Since I had no assigned duties at the firing battery positions, I started carrying shells to those positions which continued firing all day. At one point three German track vehicles came up the road from Auw. These vehicles must have been those that Major Goldstein and his bazooka teams engaged, although we had no knowledge of their actions. The howitzer in the left-hand position of A Battery was called out of the fire mission in progress and fired point blank at the tracked vehicles on the road, several hundred yards away. At one point this piece had to stop firing to allow two American soldiers to enter the battery area from the front.

In the late afternoon, Major Goldstein called for a jeep for a reconnaissance mission, and I said that I was available. He said that we would go after dark. We started out down a bare slope towards battalion headquarters, which was in a farmhouse on the road. In the darkness, I ran into some steel cable frozen into the ground. After ten minutes of my unsuccessful attempt to break free, Major Goldstein switched jeeps, and some time later a prime mover towed me out of the entangling cable. I proceeded down the hill and spent the rest of the night at battalion headquarters.

Elliott Goldstein

I was assigned to coordinate the defense of the command post. We set up an outpost forward of the command post in a house where the communications group of Headquarters Battery was stationed. Soldiers with carbines from Headquarters Battery were deployed around the area of the outpost. Two bazooka teams reported to me and were deployed on either side of the road. I took command of the personnel in the area and instructed them not to fire on tanks except on my command. At about 1400, three tanks were seen coming over the ridge on the road from Auw that led into the battalion position. Captain Huxel, the Assistant S-3, had set up an observation post in the attic of the building near which our existing observation post was set up. He attempted to adjust fire on the tanks but was unable to see the lead tank because of trees in his line of sight. When the lead tank was about two hundred yards from the outpost, it fired on a machine gun on the right of the outpost, damaging its tripod. The tank approached another fifty yards, and the tank commander opened his hatch and traversed his gun towards the outpost and fired on it. I gave the order to open fire with small arms, and the tank commander withdrew and buttoned up his hatch. The bazookas were then ordered to fire, and the gunner on the left side of the road hit the track of the lead tank.

(Unfortunately, the gunner was then hit by a shell, probably from the tank.) A Battery then fired and immobilized the tank, which burst into flames. The crew and accompanying infantry dismounted and were fired upon by a machine gun, and eliminated.

Since the bazookas were the principal defense of the battalion command post, I thought it was important that we recover the bazooka of the gunner who was killed and the rounds which he had with him. I decided to make a run for it, which meant crossing the road, and then running along a ridge to the bazooka position. I was fired on as I came to the ridge. I dove to the ground and managed to crawl to a truck rut. Fortunately for me the ground was very soft because of the snow and rain, and a prime mover which had driven across the ridge had made very deep ruts. I crawled into a deep rut on my stomach and, looking straight ahead, I saw the bazooka clutched in a bloody arm, all that was left of the man who had fired it. The sight shocked me, but I was even more disturbed when a round hit just short of the truck rut. I thought at the time it was a mortar shell, but I now believe it must have been a round from a tank. It was immediately followed by a round on the other side of the truck rut. I now knew that the German gunner had a bracket on me and that I could expect either one more adjusting round, or if the gunner thought the bracket small enough, he would lower his elevation by one half of the difference between the elevation of the over and the short, and would fire several rounds (fire for effect), assuming that one would hit the target. I accepted the fact that I was going to die, and as I stared at the bloody arm in front of me, I realized that there was nothing I could do except to pray and wait for my fate. As I expected, three shells exploded near me, all short. Fortunately, none of them scored a direct hit on the rut and the ground was soft enough so that the explosions, although close, were absorbed in the ground. As soon as I was sure that the firing had ceased, I backed down the rut with the bazooka and one round and worked my way back to the battalion observation post.

Meanwhile, Captain Huxel adjusted fire on the second tank and damaged it, and the third tank withdrew. Fire was continued on the road, adjusting the howitzers to execute a rolling barrage.

I next went with Captain Brown, commanding officer of Battery B, to assist men who had been wounded on the north of the road.

While we were helping them, one of the tanks (I believe it was the third tank) took a hull-down position behind the ridge to the east and commenced firing on personnel occupying the outpost. After directing the men on the way to the battalion aid station, Arthur Brown and I worked our way back to the battalion area, went to the attic of the building in which the observation post was located and adjusted fire on the flash of the hull-down tank. We believe that we scored a hit, since the firing ceased. If we didn't hit it, we must have convinced its commander that it would be safer to get away.

Randolph C. Pierson

For me, the morning of December 16 literally started with a bang. About 0600, I was outside the sturdy German farm house which the 589th Field Artillery Battalion was using as a command post, relieving myself in the frigid morning air at the outdoor latrine, preparatory to going on duty in the Fire Direction Center. The area northeast of us was unusually active. Squatting over the open slit trench of the latrine, with my pants around my knees, I was able to watch distant flashes of light on the horizon, and could hear the constant roll of artillery fire in the distance. This scene reminded me of early morning thunder and lightning activity I had witnessed many times during the summer months back home in central Florida.

This interesting early morning scene was cut short by the "Whoosh-Whoosh-Whoosh" sound of incoming artillery rounds. Instinctively I pulled up my pants and long johns and fell flat on the ground. The German artillery shell exploded nearby with earth-shaking power and sprayed my backsides with chunks of ice and frozen mud and filled my ears with the distinctive "Buzzzzz" of shell fragments passing above my prone body like a swarm of angry wild bees. Lying there, cold, frightened, wet and muddy, and my rear end still covered with feces, I received my introduction to the horrors of combat!

Shortly after this experience, I was on duty in the Battalion Fire Direction Center, in the relative safety of the command post, where things had gotten chaotic.

All the senior officers--Lieutenant Colonel Kelly, Major Goldstein, and Major Parker--were frantically trying to find out what was really going on. What is the situation? No one seemed to be able to find out!

The fire direction non-coms on duty, Technician Fifth Class John Celeric, Technician Fourth Class Delbert Miller, and I (Technician Fourth Class Randy Pierson), finally cornered the battalion intelligence sergeant, Technical Sergeant Frank Tacker, to get his evaluation of the situation. Frank told us he had two theories, (1) Jerry had accumulated some excess artillery ammunition and was just giving us hell in this sector, or (2) a major German attack would follow this mammoth artillery preparation. Of course, Technical Sergeant Tacker's second option turned out to be correct. History has recorded this attack as the beginning of the Battle of the Bulge.

A short time later intelligence reports trickling in led us to believe that the positions of the 589th Field Artillery Battalion would be attacked by German tanks and infantry coming from the direction of Auw, Germany, which was located to the north and east of us. However, the battalion intelligence officer, Lieutenant Joe Cocke, was concerned with a large concentration of German troops known to be in the vicinity of Prüm, Germany, to our southeast. We had lost contact with the infantry, and the Fire Direction Center was busy firing on Auw. Consequently, I was detailed to establish a listening observation post on a small secondary road that ran east, in the direction of Prüm. Two Headquarters Battery men, Private First Class Brown and Private First Class Lemley,

74

accompanied me to the location indicated on a map. "Brownie" was my radio operator, and Lemley came along to "ride shotgun" and take care of the Sarge. On the way we picked up a fourth member of the team, the battalion artillery mechanic, I remember as Corporal Fairchild.

I was instructed to look, listen, and report what we saw and heard from this position quite a distance east of the command post. We were expected to encounter one of two conditions during this mission, (1) our own infantry withdrawing, or (2) advance elements of an enemy attack. We were to report what we saw and accompany our friendly infantry back to the command post, or report and withdraw if we encountered enemy activity.

We encountered an enemy armored patrol. Against instructions, we fired a bazooka at the lead-tracked vehicle, a medium Panzer, a Panther I think, and the second bazooka round knocked off a track. The wounded Panzer effectively blocked the narrow road and the two or three following tracked vehicles immediately withdrew in the direction of Prum. Private First Class Brown was unable to contact battalion by radio to report this enemy patrol and successful action. Private First Class Lemley proved his valor and marksmanship by dispatching the Panzer crew with withering small arms fire as they tried to exit their wounded Panther.

During our engagement with the Panzer, I was slightly wounded in the face, but the three things I remember most clearly after this short but violent action are:

- The personal bravery of Private First Class Lemley;
- The professional and calm manner in which Corporal Fairchild conducted himself in this stressful and dangerous situation; and
- How afraid I was to actually fire the bazooka.

I was a patient in the station hospital at Fort Jackson, SC, a victim of spinal meningitis, when the 589" received bazooka training. My thanks to Corporal Fairchild for giving me "on the job training" in use of the bazooka. I am still proud to have hit the damned Panther twice, the only two times I have ever fired a bazooka in my life.

Arthur C. Brown

All day long we fired salvo after salvo until our guns boiled. Our battery executive officer, Ted Kiendl, went out in front of the battery to survey the situation. He was assisting in bringing in our wounded. A German assault gun had the area in its sights and was chopping up the wounded and dead with solid shot for the shock effect. As Ted brought in a wounded soldier to a log lookout post, a round of German 88 hit the shelter, spraying his face and shoulder with pieces of log. I remember his coming back to the battery dugout shouting that "nothing could live out there". He was bleeding profusely, and the blood got all over some of the letters that we'd been censoring. Ted was badly wounded and had to be evacuated, fortunately before

76

the Germans got behind us and cut off the escape routes.

Having confiscated a German "burp" gun from my forward observer, Lieutenant Cassibry, I went forward to reconnoiter. The situation was very serious, enemy tanks followed by infantry were coming straight at our gun position down the road from Auw. The Germans were in behind our infantry, having infiltrated around their exposed left flank. Lieutenant Eric Wood had succeeded in command of A Battery, as Captain Menke was captured in the first German assault. A Battery saved the day by knocking out at least one of the tanks and driving back the initial assault of enemy armor upon which they could "direct lay" one of the howitzers.

Elliott Goldstein

Ted Kiendl came up to the command post--he was still walking, although bleeding profusely. He had carried a wounded soldier back to safety. Ted was a giant of a man who had played football at Yale when football players played both defense and offense, so he was physically and mentally strong. He was put on a stretcher to be evacuated. His last words, said to me with a smile, were "Coach, I'm turning in my jockstrap. They're playing too rough out there." (Fortunately, Ted survived and returned to duty with the outfit.)

We had received orders to withdraw to a new position. Lieutenant Colonel Kelly gave me the map location of our new position and directed me to take a party with me to reconnoiter the gun positions and lead the batteries into position when they arrived. The positions were about four kilometers south of Schönberg and about the same distance (by road) southwest of our first firing positions.

Thomas P. Kelly, Jr.

It was fully dark when telephone communication with Division Artillery was restored and I received a call from General McMahon. He asked about our situation and I told him about the tank and infantry attacks, that C Battery was virtually encircled by the enemy and that we were still firing volleys into Auw but the howitzer tubes were too hot to touch and ammunition was running out. He gave the order to displace to positions west of the Schönberg-Bleialf road and to be in position and ready to register at daylight. But he warned that displacement to the rear was no guarantee of security; he understood that Bleialf was under attack and if it fell there would be no infantry to oppose an advance to Schönberg.

I gave the order to all firing batteries to cease fire and prepare to displace to the rear. But when I communicated this command by telephone to Rockwell at C Battery, he said there was no way for him to comply; all of his men were engaged in fire fights on three sides (only the south side was free of enemy infantry), and if he pulled them out in an effort to retrieve the trucks and howitzers they would all be killed. I asked if he could spare the few men necessary to disable the vehicles and destroy the howitzers

78

before evacuating and he said he would try. When I called back fifteen minutes later, the line was out. It was to be eight very long hours later before I heard again from what was left of C Battery.

There is a tenet having the force of law in the Army (as there is in the Navy) that the Commander must be the last to leave a position of danger. Although it is usually the job of the Artillery Battalion Commander to reconnoiter and assign new battery positions in the event of a displacement, in view of C Battery's disastrous situation I delegated this duty to Major Goldstein and he left with a small group from Headquarters Battery to lead the firing batteries into their new positions. I told him not to be concerned about a position for C Battery and to use the steeple of the church in Auw as the base point for registration; I wanted to be sure that every round we fired was put to good use.

I was called by Colonel Craig for an update, and I told him about C Battery's predicament and that B Battery was also under attack by ground fire, delaying its departure. He said that the 2nd Battalion of the 423rd Infantry Regiment was in Division reserve and he would talk to General Jones about releasing the Battalion to move through our area and cover our withdrawal. He also said he would ask the Colonel commanding the Corps Artillery Group to call.

Within thirty minutes I had a call from the Commander of the Corps Artillery. I told him that the Germans had tried twice to come through our area during daylight and we had repulsed them but we were pulling our howitzers out of their pits and had no way to fight them if they made another try. I also pointed out that the 590th Field Artillery Battalion was in position just west of us and was also vulnerable, as were the two regiments on the Schnee Eifel if the German forces from Auw came through us and attacked Bleialf from the north, joining forces with the Germans attacking that town from the south. The Colonel listened sympathetically and after a long pause said, "We have lots of targets to the south – I don't know if the rounds we would throw into Auw would be worth it." I said, "Well I don't know either; what is a battalion of artillery worth?" Another pause, and then, "You will be hearing from us." The firing by Corps Artillery into Auw began within twenty minutes and continued at intervals throughout the night.

We had been receiving reports from our outpost regularly until about 2100 hours when the messages stopped. I told a telephone operator to ring the outpost and he did so, but there was no answer. I took the phone and it was ringing but no one was on the line. I thought there was an even chance that the "snow troops" or other enemy infantry had captured our outpost and were on their way to the CP. I looked around and other than Major Arthur C. Parker, the Battalion S-3, the only officer in sight was 1st Lieutenant Leach, the Battalion Motor Officer, who was there as liaison with Service Battery. I told Parker to post guards around the CP and then said, "Come on, Leach, let's find out what's wrong." I drew my .45 cal. automatic and without a word he did likewise and we went out into the cold night and headed east along the snow-covered road to Auw .

I was in the lead and as we approached the barn beyond which the outpost was located I left the road to circle the barn and approach any enemy who might be hiding there from the south. As I rounded the southeast corner of the barn, I saw the problem. The telephone operator was stretched out on his sleeping bag, snoring loudly. I kicked him awake, waved my .45 in his face and told him that if he went to sleep again I would use it. Leach and I then proceeded to the outpost proper and found the three men manning it in the same outstretched posture. They received the same warning and then I told the Sergeant in command to follow me. I walked another 100 yards to the east to the German tank Goldstein and the guard had knocked out a few hours earlier and the Sergeant followed me with his automatic rifle. I said, "This is your post. The tank will give you all the cover you will need. If you see anything move, fire at it." I rejoined Leach and we went back to the CP.

I was not as tough as I sounded. About thirty minutes later the sergeant called the CP and asked to speak to me. When I answered the phone he said, "Colonel, I'll go back out there if you order me to, but it is scary as hell out there. I thought I heard somebody moaning in that tank. If you let me stay at the outpost I promise you I will not go to sleep, on my honor."

I said, "Sergeant, your honor is good enough for me." Headquarters Battery was in march order by that time, and I made sure that a vehicle and instructions were left for the outpost personnel to reach the new position before ordering the Battery to displace.

A Battery was the next to go west at about 2300 hours, slowed by the bitter cold and blackout conditions on a very dark night. B Battery was having almost as much trouble with sniper fire as C Battery and at about 2400 hours when I was despairing of saving either unit, into my CP stomped Lieutenant Colonel Joseph F. Puett, Commander of the 2nd Battalion of the 423rd. His advance guard was in trucks outside behind his command car. I tried not to show how glad I was to see him. We went outside and I showed him the area occupied by the two beleaguered batteries. He sent one platoon to that area with orders to surround the batteries and one platoon to the front to occupy both sides of the road beyond our outpost. For the first time that night I could breathe normally.

C H A P T E R IX

December 17, 1944

Thomas P. Kelly, Jr.

It was nearly 0300 hours before B Battery made its appearance; some men had been lost but all howitzers and radios were intact. The column was dispatched to its rear position, together with the outpost personnel, leaving me with my driver, Slattery (I had chosen him because he never questioned an order and rarely spoke unless asked a question), my command car and one guard armed with a carbine, together with whatever came out of C Battery's position. Puett had taken over my Command Post, but the road to Auw was quiet so I waited in the cold and the dark on the trail leading to the position of my last, remaining unit.

It was dawn before I saw shadowy figures approaching down the trail from the north. I did not have the heart to count, but there couldn't have been more than 35 survivors of a complement of nearly 100. They brought nothing out with them but their own weapons and ammunition. I told them to proceed on foot toward Bleialf and paid a last visit to my former CP to tell Puett that my unit was now displaced and that the next point of vulnerability was Radscheid, where the Headquarters and firing batteries of the 590th Field Artillery Battalion were located. I then proceeded west in my command car until I caught up with Rockwell and his group.   I dismounted and walked with him toward Radscheid.

As we walked Rockwell told me that he had carried out my order to disable his vehicles and destroy his howitzers and other equipment.   But he was despondent because of the men he had lost, including one of his lieutenants who was his best friend.   The conclusion was inescapable that he and his stragglers would not be effective as ground troops, but might be welcomed by B Battery to replace its losses.   I told Rockwell I would see him in Radscheid and went on ahead in my command car to obtain a truck from the 590th to transport him and his group to B Battery.

But when I entered the CP of the 590th I could tell that the news was bad.   The Battalion Commander, Lieutenant Colonel Vaden Lackey, whom we called the old man because he was over 40 years of age, had a sober look on his usually pleasant face.   He had sent a reconnaissance party to the Schönberg-Bleialf road and it had been fired upon by Germans, and there was a steady stream of enemy troops moving north as far as they could see, which was almost to Schönberg.   He said he had also heard by radio from Division Artillery that Schönberg was taken by Germans advancing from Andler.   His telephone lines to Division Artillery had now been severed.   Two singularly depressing facts emerged from this account: my Battalion was either captured or had made its escape through Schönberg before it fell; and what was left of the 422nd and 423rd Combat Teams was surrounded completely by strong enemy forces.

Upon his arrival at Radscheid, I advised Rockwell of the situation, telling him that he could make his own decision to stay with the 590th or to try to get out of the enemy encirclement in the direction of St. Vith where he might find the remnants of the Battalion. He chose the latter course and started north with his remaining cannoneers on the unimproved trail to the Schönberg-Bleialf road.[5] I later made an attempt to break out with my small group (I had picked up a couple of stragglers from C Battery) by another route to the northwest, but as we topped a bare ridge we came under fire from an 88 mm. gun near Wischeid and were lucky to get back to defilade on the road to Radscheid. There I rejoined Lackey. As a skilled artilleryman without a command, perhaps I could be useful to him or to the 423rd Commander, Colonel Charles C. Cavender. Without a single artillery piece I probably could not perform any useful service for my own combat team commander.

At noon on December 17, the 590th was firing rounds into Bleialf when Lackey received an order to cease firing and displace south to provide a perimeter defense for the 423rd, which had been ordered to close in to its position on the Schnee Eifel for the night. I followed Lackey in my command car from Radscheid through Oberlascheid to the Regimental Command Post east of Buchet. There we met with Cavender,

---

[5] I later learned to my deep regret that as they approached the Schönberg-Bleialf Road, Rockwell and his group were fired upon by enemy infantry and tanks; in the fire fight that followed, Rockwell and some of his men were killed, and the remainder were captured.

who was having the same problems with communications that I had experienced, but who had intermittent radio contacts with Division. He had received two messages of extreme importance: We were to receive an aerial drop of ammunition and food the next morning at specified coordinates (and the area of the drop had been surrounded by a full Company of the 1st Battalion), and the Regiment was to attack north and west across the Our River (which flowed through Schönberg) with the 422nd on our right on the following morning. However, he was unable to communicate with the 422nd to coordinate the advance, even through Division.

That night I ate my first meal, courtesy of the 423rd Headquarters Mess, in two days. I remember a conversation with Lackey, as we munched on our K rations. He said, "I'm sure you realize that we are going to be killed or captured tomorrow."

I contemplated that remark for a moment and then said, "No, I don't realize that. You can be killed or captured tomorrow if you want to, but I don't. And you will have one hell of a better chance to stay alive and free if you don't believe you'll be killed or captured."

He said, "You're just not being realistic."

I replied, "Life is the only realism I'm interested in, and I plan to hold on to it."

I also got my first sleep in two days in Cavender's German built bunker.

Calvin V. Abbott

I was a wireman in A Battery, Captain Menke's command. The first time that I remember meeting Major Goldstein was after we moved to the firing position south and west of our first position. He was in a house being used as headquarters, and we were sent there. The house was dark; the windows were covered with blankets. Major Goldstein had a map on a table and a field telephone. He told me to go into the back room and guard two women and an old man. The woman tried to get me to come over and lie on a couch or something, but I wouldn't do it. I sat in the chair with my carbine and watched them. The old man was facing me, chewing tobacco. He would spit on the floor in front of me, but the sputum never reached me. The major also instructed me that there was a young girl upstairs and that no one should be allowed to go upstairs. No one did.

After it got light, I went down to A Battery's command post and operated a telephone for Lieutenant Wood, who was commanding the battery. There was a little shack in the immediate area, and Lieutenant Wood went into it and took a nap. I don't remember the exact time, but shortly afterward a weapons carrier and jeep came down the road from the south. The men in the jeep hollered that a German tank was right behind them, so you better come on and get in the jeep. I went in the shack and woke up Lieutenant Wood and told him to come out and get in the jeep. He came out of the shack, headed down the road and started giving a firing order. I told him the guns were pulling out, or trying to. He kept on giving a firing order. The men in the jeep kept hollering, "Come on. We are the last jeep. Come on!" I pulled him by the arm and told him to come on, the jeep was going to leave us, but he kept giving orders. I ran and got in the jeep as it was moving out. That was the last time I saw him, standing in the road and calling out orders. We were the last vehicle in a group moving down the road toward Schönberg.

John R. Schaffner

The 2nd Battalion of the 423rd Infantry Regiment, in Division Reserve, was ordered to hold positions in front of the 589th while it withdrew to the rear. Meanwhile, the 589th held on in the face of heavy small arms and machine gun fire until the infantry was able to move into position shortly after midnight. About 0400 on the morning of the December 17 our battalion began to move out to the new position. By now the enemy was astride the only exit for the C Battery position so that it was unable to move. The battalion's commanding officer, Lieutenant Colonel Kelly, and his survey officer stayed behind and tried to get infantry support to help extricate this battery, but they were not fully successful. The infantry had plenty of their own problems. C Battery was never able to move its equipment and was subsequently surrounded, and almost all were killed or taken prisoner. While all this was happening, I was given orders by Captain Brown to take a bazooka and six rounds and, with Corporal Montinari, go to the road and dig in and wait

88

for the enemy attack from "that" direction. This we did and were there for some time waiting for a target to appear where the road crested. We could hear the action taking place just out of sight, but the battery was moving out before our services with the bazooka were required. As the trucks came up out of the firing position, we were given the sign to come along, so Montinari and I abandoned our hole, and bringing our bazooka and six rounds, climbed on one of the outbound trucks. I did not know it at the time, but my transfer from A Battery to B Battery was a lucky break for me, since Captain Menke, A Battery's commanding officer got himself captured right off the bat, and I probably would have been with him. A and B Batteries moved into the new position with four howitzers each, the fourth gun in A Battery not arriving until about 0730. Lieutenant Eric Wood had stayed with the last Section as it struggled to extricate the howitzer from its pit with the enemy practically breathing on them.

Battalion Headquarters Battery commenced setting up its command post in a farmhouse almost on the Belgian-German border, having arrived just before daylight. At about 0715 a call was received from Service Battery to our south, saying that they were under attack from enemy tanks and infantry and were surrounded. Shortly after that the lines went out. Immediately thereafter a truck came up the road from the south, and the driver reported enemy tanks not far behind. All communications went dead so a messenger was dispatched to tell A and B Batteries to displace to St. Vith. The batteries were notified, and A Battery with considerable difficulty got three sections on the road and started for St. Vith. The fourth howitzer again, however, was badly stuck, and while attempting to free the piece, the men came under enemy fire. The howitzer was finally gotten onto the road and proceeded toward Schönberg. Some time had elapsed before this section was able to move out.

B Battery then came under enemy fire, and its bogged down howitzers were ordered abandoned, and the personnel of the battery left the position in whatever vehicles could be moved out. I had dived headfirst out of the three-quarter ton truck that I was in when we were first fired on. In doing so, I had stuck my carbine in the snow, muzzle down. In training we were told that any obstruction of the barrel would cause the weapon to blow up in your face if you fired it. Well, I can tell you it ain't necessarily so. Under the existing circumstances, I figured I could take the chance. I just held the carbine at arms length, aimed it towards the enemy, closed my eyes and squeezed the trigger. The first round cleaned the barrel and didn't damage anything except whatever it might have hit. As the truck started moving toward the road, I scrambled into the back over the tailgate and we got the hell out of there.

Headquarters loaded into its vehicles and got out as enemy tanks were detected in the woods about one hundred yards from the battalion command post. Enemy infantry were already closing on the area. The column was disorganized. However, the vehicles got through Schönberg and continued toward St Vith. The last vehicles in the main column were fired on by small arms and tanks as they withdrew through the town. As the vehicles were passing through Schönberg on the west side, the enemy with a tank force supported by infantry was entering the town from the northeast. Before all the vehicles could get through, they came under direct enemy fire. The A Battery Executive, Lieutenant Wood, who was with the last section of the battery, almost made it through. However, his vehicle, towing a howitzer, was hit by tank fire, and he and the gun crew bailed out. Some were hit by small arms fire. Sergeant Scannipico tried to take on the tank with a bazooka and was killed in the attempt. The driver, Kenneth Knoll, also was killed there. The rest of the crew were taken prisoner, but Lieutenant Wood made good his escape. His story has been told elsewhere. Several other of the vehicles came down the road loaded with battalion personnel and were fired on before they entered the town. These people abandoned the vehicles and took to the woods, and with few exceptions were eventually captured.

Randolph C. Pierson

My second day of combat was just as traumatic as the first. We had withdrawn to our second command post location the night before, a location somewhere near a main road called the "Skyline Drive". We had hurriedly set up a fire direction center, and I had managed to grab a few winks when German tanks were reported nearby and headed in our direction.

We were given urgent orders to "Close Station-- March Order" and to proceed to St. Vith, Belgium, where the 589th was to regroup in the vicinity of the

106th Infantry Division's headquarters. We were to cross the Our River bridge, just east of the town of Schönberg, proceed with caution through Schönberg, exit the Our River valley west of Schönberg, turn south on the first main highway, and proceed to St. Vith. Good instructions, the only problem was that they were exceedingly difficult to execute.

Bedlam reigned in Headquarters Battery because the execution of our order to withdraw was accelerated by the imminent arrival of German tracked vehicles in our area from the east. During this melee, much fire direction center and personal equipment did not get loaded into the vehicles and was left to the advancing Germans.

I took it upon myself to make a last minute check of personnel. To my dismay I found Private first Class Brown slowly and methodically gathering his personal belongings and rolling up his sleeping bag. I tried to get Brownie to "pick up the cadence." My efforts were to no avail. I told Brownie he would be left behind if he did not leave with me instantly. He declined even though we could now plainly hear the advancing German armored column. In desperation, I finally left Brownie to his chores and raced to the front of the building where my transportation was supposedly waiting. The vacant space I found at the front of the building filled me with horror. All of the Headquarters Battery vehicles were gone!

The moment of truth, the moment we all dread, came swiftly and violently. I was alone, on foot, and the German armor was near. Very near! All I could do was run, and run I did. I ran as fast as I could in the ice and snow until I found the main road, turned west, and started running again. All of my instincts told me I could not outrun a German Panzer, but I was determined to try. The road ahead stretched in a straight line for what appeared to be about one mile before it made a curve into the trees. I realized I was an easy target on this long and open stretch of road; however, if I could reach the first curve without being sighted I might have a fighting chance to escape. With this in mind, I started running for my life.

I had covered some three or four hundred yards when suddenly an American three-quarter-ton Dodge truck pulled out of the woods and onto the road some three hundred yards northwest of me. I yelled at the top of my voice and vigorously waved my arms in an effort to attract the attention of the occupants of the vehicle. The effort was in vain. The vehicle continued to accelerate away from me and I continued to run and yell. Finally someone in the vehicle saw me, and the vehicle slowly rolled to a stop. Now the gap between me and the three-quarter-ton began to narrow, four hundred, three hundred, two hundred yards. I was straining, but it seemed that I would be able to reach the vehicle. Then something "spooked" the driver and the vehicle began to roll again. Now the gap began to widen, three hundred yards, four hundred yards. I was frantic! Again I yelled, waved my arms, and continued to run. My legs were weary, the muscles burning, my heart was pounding, the frigid air was stinging my lungs, I was about to collapse and give up.

A voice of authority suddenly rang out, so loud and so clear I could easily hear it at this distance, "Stop the damned truck. That's Sergeant Pierson back there!" The red brake lights came on and the Dodge skidded to a halt. With new hope in my heart and another shot of adrenaline in my blood, I ran to the vehicle and collapsed on the tailgate of the truck. Four solid, strong arms grabbed me and pulled me into the rear of the truck as the same strong voice commanded the driver to "HIT IT!"

The driver needed no further encouragement, and all four wheels of the truck spun as we gained speed, fishtailing down the icy road toward the Our River bridge. From my vantage point lying in the rear of the vehicle, I had a good view of the long, straight stretch of road behind us. As we entered the first curve in the road, several men in the vehicle let out a cheer. The last thing we observed in the distance, before we rounded the curve, seemed to be the huge black outline of a German Panzer on the road behind us.

After this date I never saw Brownie again. I still feel guilt when I think of leaving him. Brownie was more than forty years of age. He had lied about his age and "signed up" to do his part for his country. He had no sense of urgency. He was too old to be in a combat unit. What more could I have done? I have thought about it many times, and really don't know!

Much has been written and stories told about the 589th withdrawal across the Our River bridge and through the town of Schönberg on December 17, 1944. 1 believe every story I have read or heard. Anything could have happened that day! This is my personal story. The vehicle which stopped and rescued me from certain death or capture was assigned to the battalion artillery mechanic, Corporal Fairchild. For the second time in two days, he probably saved my life. He had been picking up stragglers, and I believe his was the last vehicle to leave our second position. His truck was overflowing with people and equipment. Strangely enough, the vehicle contained more men from one of the infantry regiments than it did personnel from the 589th. This fact probably got us through Schönberg.

When we approached the east bank of the Our River, we had a magnificent view of the river, Schönberg itself, and the road leaving the west side of the Our River valley. At the insistence of the infantry squad leader riding with us, we pulled the vehicle off the road and proceeded to the crest of the last hill between us and the river. There we waited and watched for what seemed to be an hour. We observed no activity whatsoever in Schönberg. For some reason, the infantry corporal felt that the north side of the town was occupied by German forces. As no one knew better, we stacked all the gear in the truck on the right, or north side, of the vehicle, providing as much protection as possible to the occupants of that side of the truck.

Finally, with bated breath and lots of caution and anxiety, we descended the hill on the eastern side of the valley of the Our River. We drew no fire until we had almost reached the Our River bridge, when a mortar crew started lobbing shells at the swiftly moving vehicle. We crossed the bridge and entered the town without getting hit. Then the infantry plan went into effect. A man with a BAR sat up front to deliver automatic fire to our front. The rest of us lay behind our barricade of gear, tarps, and bedrolls, with our weapons facing north. At each intersection in Schönberg, we fired our weapons blindly up the intersections as we passed through. There were Germans in the town. Our tactics caught them by surprise, and we made it through the town. The truck sustained superficial small arms damage. One infantryman was slightly wounded. We were very lucky!

I have no idea whether we were the first, middle, or last American vehicle to get through Schönberg. All I know is that we were alone. There were no vehicles in front of us, and we observed no vehicles behind us.

During the evening of December 17, Corporal Fairchild and I dropped the infantry squad leader and his men near the 106th Division headquarters in St. Vith, and were lucky enough to obtain fuel for the three-quarter-ton truck, food, and shelter from the cold, inclement weather. We spent an uneasy night in St. Vith among strangers, listening to sounds of battle, and wondering where the 589th was located.

Arthur C. Brown

The last vehicle out of the second gun position waited for me on the road while I checked to make sure that all personnel were clear of the position. It was now obvious that the enemy was behind our infantry in force and moving fast, there being little to stop them. When we set out for the village of Schönberg several miles to our rear, we did not realize the gravity of the situation. Although most of the trucks from A and B

Batteries got through this little town on their way back to St. Vith, by the time my truck got there, the enemy was in the town and had decided that no one else should pass. St. Vith represented a chance to regroup and fight again as it was the site of the 106th Division headquarters and a long way behind the original lines.

There was one straggler vehicle directly in front of me which I believe belonged to A Battery. This truck and ours did not make it through Schonberg. Herein lies an unbelievable episode, but it did happen. As our truck came roaring down the hill into Schonberg, shell fire was failing in and about the Our River bridge, across which we must go to get to St. Vith. I assumed that this was friendly fire falling far short of the mark because at this time I did not know the enemy had occupied the town. As we approached the bridge, some black U.S. artillerymen were running towards us and waving wildly. I thought they were just excited at the shell fire and decided in an instant to accelerate through the town and run the gauntlet. I fired my .45 pistol in the air so that they would clear the road. We turned the corner into the village, and as we passed the first house close to the road, a German tank was pulling out of the alley alongside the house. The tank was covered with hay and could have slipped in under cover of darkness and been thus camouflaged as a haystack. At any rate I still had my pistol drawn, and I emptied the clip into the gun ports of this tank, at this time only about thirty feet away. This no doubt startled the German gunner and delayed him from getting off a round from his tank gun until our vehicle was past him. His gun blast was so close that the canvas on the back of our truck bellied in.

As I looked up from this first scrape, I saw a truck on the road ahead of us that I believe was the last vehicle from A Battery in which Eric Wood was riding. Just as we came in sight, the vehicle was struck by a round from a German tank returning to Schönberg on the road from St. Vith. I ordered the driver to stop the truck, and we all jumped out into the roadside ditch. As we scattered, I ran up the hill behind a house with gunfire from small arms failing all around, and dove into a clump of bushes. After waiting for a while it was plain that no one was tracking me. Using some brush as camouflage, I slowly inched my way up the hill to the cover of some woods. In the woods I found an abandoned American tent containing some dry clothing. At this point I put on two sets of longjohns and other gear suitable for the occasion. My clothing had become drenched as I had been wallowing in the snow for some time.

Earl A. Scott

The weather on December 17 was barely flyable, but we did fly missions that morning. We received machine gun fire again, but were not hit. Instead, we watched machine gun fire being directed at a group of P-51's which were strafing the German position.

In the afternoon of December 17 we received orders to move back, and evacuated to an VIII Corps airstrip located to the rear at Beho.

Elliott Goldstein

I left our second position with the A Battery trucks and stopped in Schonberg, the location of the Division forward switching central, to call division and report our situation. Before I could do anything, word came that enemy tanks were approaching, and I left with the personnel of the switching central. We crossed the bridge safely, at high seed, and I rejoined what was left of the battalion west of St. Vith.

To understand what transpired, one must consider the direction of the German attack. Movement could only be by road, as the snow was deep and the weather cold. There were two roads coming out of the town of Auw. The north fork goes through Andler and turns south to Schönberg. The south fork, which passed through the battalion's position and along which the battalion retreated, went through Ihrenbruck into Schönberg. Since there was in fact no defending unit north of the battalion's position, the Germans were able to use one column on the south fork to attack the battalion and prevent it from firing in support of the 422nd Infantry, while they moved a second column on the north fork unopposed into Schönberg on a route almost parallel to the route that the battalion took to go into its second position. Had the battalion not moved from its second position, there would have been no escape since, in a classical double envelopment, the north arm had seized Schönberg and would prevent escape across a bridge over the Our River out of Schonberg while the south arm attacked the battalion from the rear. Of course, we could not know the big picture and did not know all of this. Had the entire situation been known, I am sure we would have been ordered initially to displace to St. Vith.

While Arthur Brown was escaping into the forest, the three howitzers of A Battery, and the bulk of Headquarters Battery, reassembled west of St. Vith, where they were joined by Service Battery of the 590th Field Artillery Battalion. Twice they were ordered into successive positions around St. Vith, but the only enemies seen were the members of a German patrol. Shortly after the group went into bivouac, the German patrol set a barn on fire one hundred yards from the bivouac.

So ended the retreat from our first and second positions. Of the twelve howitzers, only three remained. Casualties had been heavy, and many officers and men had been killed, wounded and captured. We were no longer a battalion, but more like a small task force made up of the remaining personnel of A and B Batteries, Headquarters Battery and a Service Battery.

CHAPTER X

December 18, 1944

Thomas P. Kelly, Jr.

The next morning after breakfast there was a long wait for the aerial drop, which never came. At about 1000 hours the Combat Team began its march north. The 2nd Battalion, which had closed into the area of Oberlasheid on the 17th, was in the lead and ran into German troops advancing northeast from Bleialf toward Radscheid at noon. Cavender ordered an attack to clear his route through that village and a battle ensued in which Puett's unit was supported by howitzers (the artillery pieces) of the 590th. Feeling particularly helpless without any means of contributing to the defeat of the enemy, I drove to a high point near the junction of the road to Bleialf with the roads to Schönberg and Radscheid where I could watch the engagement. It appeared that neither side was prevailing until late in the afternoon when Lackey, who was running short of ammunition, began using white phosphorus projectiles.[6] The effect was

---

[6] When these shells burst they not only created an immediate dense cloud of smoke, making vision impossible, but threw out thousands of particles of burning phosphorus which would instantly burn through clothing and even boots, and the flesh underneath.

immediate and devastating: The enemy withdrew beyond the Schönberg-Bleialf road.

During the battle the 3rd Battalion moved north through Radscheid and along the unimproved road toward Schönberg (the trail that Rockwell and his remnant had taken), while the 1st Battalion relieved the 2nd in contact with the enemy. I joined with Cavender at his Headquarters in Radscheid after dark (he was in the same building that was Lackey's CP until the day before). He had lost contact with the Commander of the 3rd Battalion, Lieutenant Colonel Earl F. Klinck, and I was with him when he ordered a communications sergeant to lay a wire to the north until he found the Battalion CP. I was advised by Cavender that a new order had been received from Division to attack Schönberg in the morning and that the 3rd Battalion was to lead the attack. I asked if I could go with the wire detail and perhaps counsel with Klinck about the use of the 590th in his attack. Permission was granted.

Before we started north the communications sergeant told me that Cavender had sent him down the road to Auw in an effort to make contact with the 422nd and lay a wire into its Headquarters. He said that about one mile down the road a German with a blazing burp gun had appeared at the side of the road. One of his men had killed the German with his automatic rifle, but not knowing how many of the enemy were around, they had beat a hasty retreat. We then started north in our two vehicles; presumably in deference to my rank the sergeant had waved me into the lead. But as we proceeded through extreme darkness with dense woods on both sides of the roadway, I remembered the sergeant's account of his recent experience. I had drawn my .45 and the soldier sitting beside me in the front seat of my command car had his carbine at the ready, but we would be no match for a burp gun in the woods.

I ordered Slattery to stop and I got out of the command car and walked back to the wire truck. I said to the Sergeant, "You guys are much better armed than we are, why don't you go first?"

The sergeant's immediate reply, "I don't like anybody following me when I'm laying wire. You might get tangled in the wire or at least damage it."

My response, "Then your two automatic riflemen will ride with me on the running boards of my command car."

The sergeant started, "But these are my men. . . " .

I interrupted, "That is an order, sergeant." There was a long pause and then a salute by the sergeant (tinged, I thought, with mockery) who nodded to the two riflemen. I felt much better with one of them on each side of my command car, but I held on to my .45.

We proceeded to a left turn in the road that I knew would take us to the Schönberg-Bleialf road. But there were tracks continuing north and the sergeant and I agreed that they were made by vehicles of the 3rd Battalion. We continued north, following the tracks through the darkness, until we reached a small valley or hollow in which we began to make out the shapes of vehicles. I dismounted and walked ahead of my command car; the vehicles were indeed those of the 3rd Battalion and every driver and all other personnel in the trucks were asleep. I thought, "What a nice surprise party for the Germans", who were in strength along the main road less than a kilometer to the west.

I made out a sharp rise to the north and correctly guessed that Klinck had established his CP there. I showed Slattery where I wanted him to park my command car and then proceeded up the slope a distance of about 200 yards, where I found Klinck.

He informed me that he was to lead the attack on Schönberg in the morning, supported by the other two Battalions on his left. From his map he estimated the distance to Schönberg to be 1 1/2 kilometers (about one mile) and mostly down hill. He understood that there would be an aerial drop of ammunition and food, both of which were in short supply, on his position soon after daybreak. I assured him, from my conversations with Cavender, that the other two Battalions and the 590th were on their way north and would close in on his position during the night. This was confirmed a few minutes later by Cavender himself, telephone communications having now been established by the wire truck that had followed me to the position.

I made a trip to my command car to get my bedroll and found Slattery and the guard asleep in their seats. It was then only a few hours before dawn so I decided against the bedroll, which I hadn't used since the first night in the bivouac area near St. Vith. I could hear many vehicles closing into the hollow to the south and correctly assumed that the remaining units of the Combat Team were arriving for the attack. I went back up the hill, found a patch of ground without snow or ice and sat against a tree, waiting for dawn and nodding from time to time.

Earl A. Scott

On December 18 all of the VIII Corps pilots, including the pilots assigned to each of the 106th Division field artillery units, were ordered to fly to the VIII Corps airstrip near Bastogne. The ceiling was zero and the time was 1530. Two planes were without pilots and Lieutenant Cassibry, my observer, volunteered to fly one of them out. He had never flown an L-4 but had received some flying training at an Army training school until he cranked a plane with no one in it. It took off and crashed over the end of the runway. At this point, the school had sent him back to us. But on this afternoon he flew a plane out.

I followed him into the air and quickly flew into a solid fog bank. I tried a lower level, but the fog there was very heavy. Deciding to gain altitude and return to the airstrip at Cherain, I found heavy fog there also. In the process of climbing, suddenly Cassibry sailed across my front--I barely missed crashing into him. At this point I decided that he would not make it and gave myself a very slim chance. My parachute was on a shelf behind me or else it would have been my first jump. Fortunately, that summer I had taken a three-week course in instrument and night flying. With this knowledge I decided to spiral down and hopefully come out of the fog before crashing. When one hundred feet was indicated on my altimeter, I was out of the fog and over a field large enough to land. There at the edge of the field along a concrete highway stood a lone American soldier. I landed, and as I taxied up to the road, the soldier came over to me. He was actually a chaplain. Just what I needed! He told me that Bastogne was just about four miles down the highway; he had just come from there, and it wasn't too foggy. I proceeded to fly down the highway and very shortly was over Bastogne. The airstrip could not be found because of heavy fog. I then realized that darkness was setting in. In the near total darkness I landed in a field located about a half mile west of Bastogne. Somehow, Cassibry also made it to Bastogne and lived to fly again.

Randolph C. Pierson

On the morning of December 18, I found a mess truck and a friendly mess sergeant who agreed to feed us coffee, bread, and hot-cooked cereal. While Corporal Fairchild and I were eating, we were approached by an officer I did not recognize. He was rounding up stragglers and wanted us to join his group in establishing a roadblock nearby. I promptly advised him we were members of the 589th Field Artillery Battalion and it was our duty to find and return to that unit. The officer did not like my answer, but he did give us a location where he thought the 589th might be found. I thanked him for the information and Corporal Fairchild and I finished our meal quickly so we could be on our way. When we thanked the mess sergeant for his hospitality, he grinned and told me he was glad I "stood up" to that rear echelon officer. He wished us good luck and shoved some C rations and cigarettes at us as we left, just in case we couldn't find our unit right away.

The remainder of December 18 was spent searching for the unit and bucking traffic. We always seemed to be heading in the direction opposite to that of the majority of the traffic, which was away from the sounds of battle. We stopped frequently, asking questions of people whom we thought could help us locate the the 589th. On one occasion a group of American stragglers, headed in the direction opposite to ours, blocked the road, stopped us, and tried to commandeer the truck at gunpoint. Both Fairchild and I leveled our weapons at the senior noncom in the group and told him he would be the first to die if they tried to take our truck. This was a touchy situation because we were outmanned and outgunned, but I meant what I said. I would have shot him between the eyes before I would have turned the truck over to them. Fortunately for all, the group backed down and let us resume our journey.

By nightfall we had not found any personnel of the 589th and joined a small group of tracked vehicles who were in bivouac just off of the road. Again we were lucky; they fed us some ten-in-one rations and allowed us to curl up in the back of our truck for the rest of the night.

Elliott Goldstein

The German breakthrough immediately put advancing columns on roads west of the lines of at least three American divisions. On December 18 the higher commands finally commenced reacting to the threat. Since the 106th Division had been penetrated and practically rendered ineffective, it could not be utilized as an infantry division, but Division Headquarters and the 424th Infantry Regiment were assigned to defend St. Vith. Remnants of other units were used to plug holes on a temporary basis. The group from the 589th Field Artillery Battalion was ordered to take successive defensive positions along roads on which the Germans could be expected to advance, to act as an anti-tank defense, and eventually was ordered to take a position near Bovigny. There it was attached to the 174th Field Artillery Group and, with the aid of observers from that group, prepared for indirect fire.

To reach Bovigny, we had taken a circuitous route, proceeding south as far as the principality of Luxembourg, then turning north, and taking positions along the way. This involved a lot of backing and filling, so that we were actually moving in circles. The roads were crowded with troops moving into defensive positions. As we were engaged in these ventures, a convoy of jeeps drove up. The second vehicle was occupied by a driver and a three-star general, with hand grenades hanging from either side of his cartridge belt suspenders. It was Lieutenant General Ridgeway, commander of the XVIII Airborne Corps. Our conversation was short. He said, "Who the hell is in command of these guns?" I gave my best salute and said, "I am, sir!" He replied, "Get those damn guns off the road!" I gave my standard reply to higher ranking

108

officers -- "Yes, sir!" And off the road and into the ditch we went. Neither of us could know at the time how important those three howitzers were to become to his defense.

CHAPTER XI

December 19, 1944

Thomas P. Kelly, Jr.

December 19 was the first reasonably clear day I had seen in Germany. I thought surely the promised drop would be made, but it was not. Neither were orders received to cancel the attack. Instead Cavender received a garbled message from Division calling upon every man to do his duty in somewhat dramatic language that I considered unnecessary and uncalled for. Commanders of all units assembled on the hill where Cavender had now established his Headquarters at about 0800 hours and a detailed order for the attack was given by Cavender and his Executive Officer, Lieutenant Colonel Fred W. Nagle. The 3rd Battalion was to begin its advance at 1000 hours, supported by the 2nd Battalion on its left and the 1st Battalion on the extreme left, along the Schonberg-Bleialf road. Although short of ammunition the 590th would provide artillery support from positions south and east of the high ground on which we stood.

At that moment we heard artillery firing in the west and then heard the whine of projectiles overhead. Fortunately, the shells fell 100 yards beyond the point where we were assembled, but tree bursts made our position very uncomfortable. I saw a slit trench and dived into it, as did many others. When I looked up I saw the white, tense face of a corporal. "Is this your

111

slit trench?", I asked; the corporal nodded. Shells were still falling in the trees just beyond us. I got up, pushed the corporal into the trench and jumped in on top of him. My back was at ground level, but he was very secure.

After four or five salvos the shells stopped and I bounced out of the trench. Immediately there were hundreds of guttural shouts and massive small arms fire from the hollow south of the hill. This could mean only one thing: the enemy had attacked the rear echelon including all of the vehicles and drivers of the combat team. I wondered about my faithful Slattery and said a little prayer. Then I remembered that in my bedroll was a bottle of Old Forrester, my favorite bourbon, that I had brought from the states and had resolved not to open until the Germans finally surrendered, at which point I had planned to drink it all in one sitting. I consoled myself with the thought that the way things were going, the Germans might never surrender.

Cavender was giving orders to his Battalion Commanders designed to protect the troops forming for the attack on Schönberg from the enemy in the rear, thus depleting his forces for the attack. I looked for and found Lackey and asked him if his batteries had gone into position to support the attack or if they were overrun by the enemy in the hollow. He looked at me with ashen face and said he was afraid they were lost; he had delayed the order to occupy gun positions until he had heard Cavender's orders for the attack. So the depleted and outnumbered 423rd would attack entrenched forces of the enemy, reinforced with artillery and armor, without artillery fire support or sufficient ammunition to sustain the attack. The hopelessness of the situation was apparent to everyone.

I waited until Cavender had given orders to, and had dispatched, all of his officers, including the very competent Nagle. I then approached him and said that it appeared that he would not have artillery support and, therefore, any hope that I might have assisted in the attack had vanished. He agreed. I asked if he knew the location of the 422nd, because I felt it was my duty to join my own combat team if I could not be of any use to him. Again, he agreed, but knew only what he had learned from one of his patrols earlier that morning: the 422nd was advancing on Schönberg from positions south and east of his regiment. I wished him luck in his attack but he managed only a weak smile and a shake of the head.

I said goodbye to Lackey and struck out down the hill in a southeasterly direction. Now I was really alone. The area in which I found myself was strangely quiet, almost eerie in its complete silence. There were birds and squirrels in the trees and a few rabbits in the brush, apparently oblivious to the presence of thousands of armed men all around them bent upon each other's destruction. I saw a figure on a hillside 150 yards to my right, heard the crack of a rifle and a sound very like that of an angry hornet go past my ear. I dived into a clump of bushes and crawled from there into a copse of pine trees. I looked back and the figure was gone so I proceeded in a southeasterly direction as defined by the hand compass I always carried.

I was fired at twice more without knowing where the shots were coming from and was becoming skittish. When I heard the tramp of feet approaching through dense forest I again dove into underbrush and looked out under the branches and leaves in the direction of the sound. To my great relief I saw GI combat boots. I waited until they had passed and then rose up out of the brush and said, "Don't shoot. I'm Lieutenant Colonel Kelly, Commander of the 589th Field Artillery and I'm looking for the 422nd Headquarters." The sergeant commanding the patrol said, "We're going in that direction, Sir, follow us."

There was firing ahead of us that grew louder and sharper as we proceeded. We detoured around several fire fights involving burp guns and light machine guns of the enemy and automatic rifles and .50 caliber machine guns of the 422nd. I heard mortar fire, but was to learn that it must have been German; the 422nd had exhausted its supply of mortar shells. Finally, the sergeant pointed to a tent in a clearing on a hillside and then continued his route. I made my way to the tent.

It was about 1500 hours when I first saw Descheneaux at his Headquarters. He was distraught and appeared close to tears. He said he was glad I was still alive and only hoped we both would live through this. He said he had been promised aerial drops that had not happened, was out of food and running short of ammunition of all calibers. I told him I had been with the 423rd Combat team and described its situation. He said he was sorry that the two regiments couldn't help each other. As we talked we were standing outside his Headquarters tent and the Medical Aid

Station was only about 75 yards away. Every time a wounded man was carried by on the way to the Station, Descheneaux looked at him and became a little more teary.

I left him to dig a slit trench beside the Headquarters tent. I grabbed a shovel and had broken ground and made some progress when I saw an officer (I believe it was Lieutenant Colonel Joseph Matthews, Jr., the regimental Executive Officer, but at this time I am not certain) run by me with a large white object that looked like an undershirt. I thought it was odd, but when he continued to run north, in the direction of the Germans, it came to me. He was carrying a flag of truce and intended to surrender us to the enemy.

I dropped my shovel and ran back to where I had left Descheneaux. "You can't surrender, Desch," I said. "If you hold out for about two more hours, a lot of us can try to get out to the west tonight." Descheneaux said, "What else can I do? I don't want to be responsible for any more killing. Our situation is hopeless, why go on getting men killed?" Then he turned away and shouted an order: "All of you destroy your weapons, now! Cease fire, now! Call in your units and line them up on the road to the north!" Then he put his hands over his face and cried unashamedly.

I turned away and broke my .45 on a rock. I had sworn I would never again be captured; it had happened once on maneuvers in Tennessee and I had escaped. I swore at that moment that I would escape again. I followed Descheneaux and his staff to the head of a rapidly growing group of solemn and unarmed American infantrymen, facing to the north and surrounded by heavily armed German troops.

When the German Captain in command of our captors was satisfied that the remaining able-bodied personnel of the 422nd Infantry Regiment were assembled and unarmed, dusk was approaching. We were ordered by the Captain (who was able to speak in what we came to understand was the German version of the English language) to form a column facing north. The German soldiers guarding us on both sides were unable to speak any derivation of English, so all commands had to be passed back from the head of the column by our own men. In this manner the approximately two thousand enlisted men and officers who had responded to the order to surrender were directed to move north, and upon reaching the Andler-Auw Road were turned east.

The road was jammed with German infantry and vehicles, including tiger and panther tanks, moving west. Their progress was slow due to the congestion (to which we contributed our share, although we wisely yielded the right-of-way to the armed enemy), but all of us were impressed with the mighty forces that the Germans were pouring into a sector that the Americans were wholly unprepared to defend. As I trudged through the snow, which was knee deep in the off-the-road areas not pre-empted by the enemy columns, looking up through the dusk at the tigers and panthers and the scowling faces protruding from their turrets, it required all of my remaining fortitude and resolve to overcome despair. But once the internal battle was won, I was more than ever determined to see it through.

By the time we reached Auw, darkness had fallen and we were interned in several buildings that served as the village school. We were informed that food would be provided, and although we waited several hours before the lights were extinguished and we could sleep, nothing edible made its appearance. We were to learn that the promise of sustenance was one that the Germans took very lightly, and was usually made as a means of maintaining control. The subsequent excuses for nonperformance were varied and frequently ingenious. In this instance, as I recall, the ration trucks were delayed and didn't arrive due to American artillery fire.

Elliott Goldstein

We had gone into position near Bovigny in the dark on the night of December 18, and had fired a few missions during the night using a map for direction. The next morning we attempted to register one of the pieces. Several rounds were fired, but no one could see them. The officer conducting fire, an officer of the 174th Field Artillery Group, ordered a smoke shell but couldn't see the burst. He then ordered the fuse set for a high burst. When the round was fired, the telephone operator, who was looking at the officer, shouted, "Look back there!" Immediately behind us we saw the smoke drifting down. In the night, the officer at the howitzers had apparently become disoriented, and had laid them 180 degrees out of the setting ordered. The

117

error was quickly corrected, the pieces were turned around, and we registered, which enabled us to report "Ready" to the 174th Field Artillery.

As a footnote, we learned that during the night the Division rear echelon heard artillery fire coming towards them, and assumed they were being attacked. All personnel were ordered out to form a defensive line along a ridge. Since the ridge curved, instead of forming a straight line, they formed a "U". Nothing happened until one of the clerks was spooked by something in the night and fired at it. Unfortunately, he was firing at the other end of the line, and everyone started firing--at each other. Fortunately, no one was hit. We heard the story when we reached Vielsalm, but we didn't tell them what we assumed had brought it about.

At about 1100 on December 19, the 174th Field Artillery Group prepared to move north through Salmchateau to the northwest, and the 589th was ordered to go into bivouac near Salmchateau for reorganization.

Meanwhile, the remnants of Headquarters Battery and Service Battery of the 590th Field Artillery and the entire 592nd Field Artillery, with a full complement of men and guns, withdrew towards March. (The after action report indicated that this was not on the orders of higher authority, and having served under Lieutenant Colonel Richard Weber, a regular Army officer who commanded the 592nd, I think I know how his mind worked. He undoubtedly concluded that there was no military reason or utility for a 155-howitzer unit to attempt direct fire so, on his own initiative, he

118

withdrew his unit to the west where he eventually set up for indirect fire in support of the overall effort.)

Randolph C. Pierson

About noon on December 19, we found part of the 589th near Salmchateau. Corporal Fairchild dropped me off at Headquarters Battery and left quickly when he found out Service Battery was in bivouac near Vielsalm. I rejoined the fire direction team just in time to make the journey to the crossroads at Baraque de Fraiture.

I remember thinking this was a terrible way to spend my twenty-first birthday, heading north to fight Panzers again. Major Parker, now commanding the battalion, received orders to split the reduced battalion into two elements: one element to move west and establish a defensive roadblock in a village I had never heard of and the second element to move west to the crossroads located at Baraque de Fraiture, Belgium, to repel an expected Panzer attack. I was assigned to the advance party of the second element and arrived at Baraque de Fraiture at about 1400 hours. My responsibility was to help establish the command post, fire direction center, message center, and a local communication network. Frankly, I was perplexed and angry that an already beat-up artillery outfit was being given the job of fighting Panzers, nor could I comprehend why Panzers would attack here. Before we arrived, there was nothing to attack but three or four empty buildings and a few milk cows. I couldn't understand why the German army would fight for this

119

bleak, windswept, cold, snow-covered, open spot in the Ardennes Forest. I was concerned that we had not seen our commanding officer, Lieutenant Colonel Thomas P. Kelly Jr., in three days. No one knew what had happened to him.

CHAPTER XII

December 20, 1944

Thomas P. Kelly, Jr.

We were aroused in Auw by our German escort on the morning of December 20, and were permitted a very brief and extremely crowded interlude for our morning toilette before we were ordered into the street. We left Auw shortly after daybreak and walked the snow-covered road to Prum (which had been one of our earlier artillery targets), reaching that town in early afternoon. We then turned east and followed a road from which some of the snow had been removed. Shortly thereafter, we were walking past a field of potatoes on the north side of the road and two of the younger officers, who undoubtedly had not eaten in two days, ran into the field to harvest a small portion of the crop. Immediately shots rang out from the German guards along the column and one of the Americans was hit. However, he was fortunately not seriously wounded, and he and his companion ran back to the road. There were no more deviations from the designated route of march.

I do not know how far we walked that day, our journey punctuated by brief rest stops, but it probably exceeded thirty kilometers (over twenty miles). There were some who fell out due to fatigue induced by minor wounds or other injuries and lack of food. I refused to speculate concerning their disposition, but

121

the memory of the two soldiers who had broken ranks to gather potatoes was fresh in my mind.

At dusk we arrived at a picturesque little town that we were informed was Gerolstein. The old buildings of typical German design occupied a narrow valley with wooded slopes rising abruptly on both sides of the main street and the railroad track. Finally, that night food was provided in the form of black bread, dry crackers and half cooked potatoes. It was hardly a feast but it was attacked with great vigor by the young soldiers and junior officers. We did not intercede to obtain our share until it appeared that it would vanish before we had an opportunity to do so. Even then our participation was minimal and far from satisfying. We would grow accustomed to this feeling of a lack of fulfillment in every aspect of our lives.

I noticed that night, and increasingly with the passage of time, that a metamorphosis was occurring in the younger men, officers and enlisted men alike. While I did not have an opportunity to observe many of them in combat, those I had been in contact with, including the detachment who had escorted me to the Regimental CP, and those I observed in fire fights with Germans on the way, were not lacking in courage or determination; even when forced to give up their arms they were belligerent and rebellious toward their captors. But there was something about being prisoners of the Germans, about losing their weapons and being completely in the power of the despised enemy, that seemed to deprive them of all spirit and inner strength. Some whom I had seen exhibit courage in the face of enemy fire now cowered in corners, and personal safety, which had been a secondary consideration just a few days earlier, now dominated their behavior. I now understand why released prisoners of war are not immediately returned to combat; they require rehabilitation and reindoctrination to become again competent soldiers.

Elliott Goldstein

The 589th Group received orders from General McMahon on December 20, to move toward Baraque de Fraiture to defend against a possible tank attack from that direction, and to protect the supply line to Vielsalm where at that time the 106th Division Rear headquarters was located. Near Baraque de Fraiture two howitzers were placed about five hundred yards west of the crossroads and laid to the east. The remaining howitzer was placed at the crossroads and laid to the south. No attack materialized, and the group organized a perimeter defense and went into bivouac for the night. No rations had been received except for emergency rations contributed by the 174th Field Artillery Group. Gasoline and ammunition were low. Trucks were sent into Vielsalm for rations, ammunition and gasoline. Some supplies were received, and we received orders to move closer to Vielsalm in order to draw equipment and supplies and reorganize. While we were in preparation, we received an additional five men and supplies from Division rear echelon at Vielsalm, and orders from General McMahon (I believe by radio) to set up a roadblock at Baraque de Fraiture to protect the Division's supply routes from the south and west.

Charles P. Jacelon

Early on the morning of December 20, we started out for Vielsalm. I was driving the lead jeep with Major Parker in the passenger seat. As we reached a point where our road crossed another, a two and a half-ton Army truck came speeding toward us on the other road from the direction of Houffalize. Major Parker yelled, "Whoa," and I stopped the jeep. The Major got out and asked the driver of the truck where he was going in such a hurry. The driver said that a German tank attack was heading our way from Houffalize. By this time Major Goldstein had walked up from his jeep, which was following ours, and he said, "You know, we came over here to fight a war and this looks like a good place to start." Major Parker said, "I was thinking the same thing, Major, set up for the defense of this crossroad." Major Goldstein said, "I am going to ask my big friend here (a track vehicle with a bulldozer blade) to dig me some gun pits."

This is the true verbatim conversation that led to the story of Parker's Crossroads. I believe that initially Major Parker entered the building that became Captain Brown's command post. The building had a bar, and while Major Parker was doing his planning and mapwork by flashlight, someone handed him a bottle of beer that had been found in the basement. Major Parker drank half, then handed it to me saying, "Here, driver, I want you to have some of this." A young woman resident rushed in to get something from a drawer or a cabinet, and Major Parker said to her, "You don't have to leave, we'll protect you." Her reply was, "Boche come, I go", and she left.

Elliott Goldstein

That conversation between Major Parker and me, and my actions thereafter, seem insane today when considered out of context. However, both Arthur Parker and I were sick of running. We had been chased out of our first and second gun positions and for two days had been wandering from one position to another, going into position to counter threats of attack and then moving on again. Neither of us wanted ever again to be attacked in a defenseless position. That is the reason we decided to do more than set up the "roadblock" ordered by General McMahon; we were determined to establish a fortified position at Baraque de Fraiture in order to be able to defend against the attack of which the fleeing truck driver had warned us, and hopefully any other attack.

What we didn't know was that two German divisions had been assigned to attack along the axis of the Houffalize-Bastogne Road towards Liege, proceeding north with the ultimate objective, by a sweep behind the Allies' rear, of cutting off the supplies coming from Antwerp and Amsterdam. One of the German divisions was the crack Second S.S. Panzer Division. Our intelligence capacity was severely limited by our lack of reliable communications. All we knew was that we very likely would be attacked in this position, and we were determined to protect ourselves in the event of attack from any direction except from Manhay, which was not in enemy hands.

Two tanks from the 7th Armored Division came into our area, in addition to the observer who adjusted fire on Samree. We were also joined by four vehicles from the 203rd Armored Anti-Aircraft Battalion, three of which were armed with four 50-caliber machine guns and one which was a self-propelled 37-millimeter gun. This group had been driven out of position south of the crossroads. We asked that they join us, and they agreed. At Major Parker's direction, we made plans for coordination of fire for all weapons, and lines of direction of fire were staked out on the ground. Outposts were placed five hundred yards out to the west, south, and east. Telephone lines were strung to each of the outposts. In addition, a daisy chain of mines was laid across the road from the south near the southern outpost.

John R. Schaffner

I didn't even know who was in charge of the rag-tag group that I was with until I saw Major Goldstein out in the open verbally bombasting the enemy (wherever they were) with all the curse words he could think of, and at the top of his booming voice. I thought that he wouldn't be around too long if there were any Germans out there to hear him. Apparently, there were none, since he didn't draw any fire. As for me, I was taking cover behind the rear wheel of one of our trucks, and felt rather naked.

The three howitzers were ordered into position to defend the crossroads, and I was told to go out "there" and dig in and took for an attack from "that" direction, still having no idea of the situation. Most of the night was spent in the foxhole. All was quiet on the front line. When I was relieved during the night to get some rest, I tried to find a dry place in the stone barn to lay down. The floor was deep in muck, but the hayrack on the wall was full of dry hay so I accepted that as a good place to sleep. Pushing the cows aside, I climbed into the hay. I guess that the cows just didn't understand because they kept pulling the hay out from under me until I was to become the next course on their menu. However, it wasn't long before I was outside in another hole in the ground.

Harold L. Kuizema

There was snow on the ground; it was cold and so foggy that it was impossible to see more than one hundred feet. Late in the afternoon, we arrived and set up our three 105-millimeter howitzers just beyond Parker's Crossroads. South of the crossroads a few rounds were fired by A Battery's howitzer. When things quieted down, some of my 589th buddies felt it was necessary to clean up and shave. For me shaving was not a priority since I had very little beard growth at that time. Soon the order came to go into positions to defend the crossroads (Baraque de Fraiture). We took over some of the larger family homes there. The

127

home we took over had an attached barn with cows and hay to feed the cows. The elderly gentleman whose home we took over had taken the time to milk the cows before he left. As he left he offered me some milk, which I refused; I'm not sure why since that was to be the last time we saw fresh milk for an extended period. The picture of his walking off with his little pushcart containing his belongings is still very vivid in my mind.

We all found a variety of places to sleep in this house. There was always someone who pulled guard. My memory says we were on guard two hours and then off for four hours. I don't recall sleeping much there. My buddy Bernard Strohmier remembers sleeping on the hay in the barn.

In the morning, we positioned ourselves around the house. My buddies were busy laying land mines across the road. Others had set up the machine guns. We placed our trucks, which were weapon carriers, and used them for protection and defense. We lay right underneath the trucks with our weapons.

CHAPTER XIII

The Battle of Parker's Crossroads Begins

Elliott Goldstein

Arthur Brown managed to evade capture by the Germans, came through their lines leading a number of others who had similarly evaded capture and, with the help of a Belgian farmer, came back through the American lines. Arthur asked to be taken to Vielsalm, the rear headquarters of the 106th Division. There he found Major Parker who had come back to Vielsalm for supplies and ammunition.

He declined Major Parker's offer to retire for rest and recuperation. "I was mad at what was being done to our side and itching to get back in the fight, now having a few chips stacked on my side." After refitting he came back to Baraque de Fraiture.

Without discussing the command structure, we each took the position where we were most capable and needed. Major Parker took command and also acted as S-3, in coordinating fire. Captains Brown and Huxel commanded the three howitzers, and I coordinated the defense of the area. I placed defensive positions around our perimeter and assigned positions for those men who were not in the howitzer crews. One tank-mounted, 50-caliber machine gun was placed to fire down the road to the south and the other 50 calibers were distributed around to protect the outposts. The area was defended to the best of our ability with our equipment, but it was hardly a strongly fortified position. We did not believe we would remain there very long--only long enough for relief to arrive.

It's hard to realize today just how severe were the conditions under which we had to operate. The temperature was always below freezing; there was heavy fog and cloud cover. No air support was available. Snow was heavy, and the only way to move quickly was on the roads. While the weather aided us by making it almost impossible for tanks to move anywhere except on the roads, it made survival difficult. Everyone was subject to frostbite and frozen hands and feet. Our shoes were not waterproof and if our feet got wet and were not dried, they were damaged by trench foot, a breakdown of the blood vessels in the feet, which could result in loss of a foot.

I didn't have much faith in my .45-caliber pistol in the situation we were in. A lieutenant from the 7th Armored and I were talking about the conditions facing us, and he said he'd like to have my .45. I told him I'd swap it and my jacket for his Thompson sub-machine gun (tommy gun) and his jacket, which was warmer than mine. He was glad to do it, he said, because if his tank were hit, the crew had to bail out through the turret, and the tommy gun often got caught and had to be abandoned. I felt a lot more secure with the tommy gun, and he was happy to have a weapon he could hang on his belt and take with him if he had to get out of his tank in a hurry.

Food was in short supply, and I think we kept going on adrenaline. The rush of adrenaline provided energy and anger gave us all courage. We used one house as a command post and both houses as shelter from the cold. An observation post was set up in the second story of the command post, and the principal radio was placed in the cellar.

John R. Schaffner

The weather remained miserable, cold, wet, and foggy with a little more snow for good measure. If the enemy was around, he was keeping it a secret. The day went very slowly. (This kind of time is usually spent getting your hole just a bit deeper, you never know how deep is going to be deep enough.) Now and then one of our guys would pop off a few rounds at something, real or imagined.

We were joined by some AAA people with a towed trailer mounted with four .50-caliber machine guns and a 37-millimeter cannon. I thought at the time I'd hate to be in front of that thing when it went off. (I only saw the one unit then, but the books reporting the action mention that there were four of these units there from the 203rd AAA, 7th Armored Division.) This weapon was positioned to fire directly down the road to Houffalize. Frank Aspinwall also reports that we were joined by a platoon of the 87th Recon Squadron.

Later in the evening, Captain Brown sent me with another B Battery GI, Ken Sewell, to a foxhole in the ditch at one side of the road to Houffalize, about a couple of hundred yards out from the crossroads (hard to remember exactly). We were the outpost and had a field telephone hookup to Captain Brown's command post. Captain Brown told us to just sit tight and report any movement we observed. There was a "daisy chain" of mines strung across the road a few yards ahead of our position to stop any vehicles. The darkness was made even deeper by the thick fog that night, with a silence to match. Now and then a pine tree would drop some snow or pine cone or make some other noise. I think my eyelids and ears were set on "Full Open."

There we sat in this hole in the ground just waiting and watching, until about midnight when we could hear strange noises in the fog. It was very dark and our visibility was extremely limited, but we were able to discern that what was making the strange noise was about a dozen Germans who came into view on bicycles. They stopped in the road when they came to the mines. Being unaware of our presence, not ten yards away, they stood there in front of us in the middle of the road--probably talking over what to do next. We could hear that the language was not English and they were wearing "square" helmets. Sewell and I were in big trouble. This was a first for us to be this close to the enemy. Thinking that there were too many for us to take on with our carbines, I took the telephone and whispered our situation to Captain Brown. His orders were to "Keep your head down and when you hear me fire my .45 the first time we will sweep the road with AAA quad 50's. When that stops, I'll fire my .45 again, and then we will hold fire while you two come out of your hole and return to the command post. Make it quick!"

And that's the way it happened. That German patrol never knew what hit them. On hearing the .45 the second time Ken and I left our hole and keeping low, ran back toward our perimeter. I was running so hard that my helmet bounced off my head and went rolling out into the darkness. I thought, "to hell with it" and never slowed down to retrieve it. I lost sight of Ken and honestly don't remember seeing him again. I heard many years later that he was captured along with Bernard Strohmier and others after the Germans took the crossroads.

By calling out the password "Coleman" I got safely past our perimeter defense and was then shot at (and missed) by somebody at the howitzer position as I approached it. After a blast of good old American obscenities, they allowed me through and I reported to Captain Brown. (The official book says that there was an eighty man patrol from the 560th Volks Grenadier Division and 2nd Panzer Division out there that night. Maybe the rest were back in the fog somewhere.)

Arthur C. Brown

Being the only firing battery commander to make it out of the first gun position on December 17, my assignment was to take charge of the three A Battery guns at what has now been named Parker's Crossroads. Our howitzers were trained down every road except for the northwest, which was then supposed to be the friendly rear. This unguarded road led to Manhay, which later turned out to be the scene of two battles. I took up position on the southwest corner of the crossroads on the road to the south leading to Houffalize, and near the road leading to Samree, which was on the road to Salmchateau and Laroche. Now the

133

words "Baraque de Fraiture" mean "barracks in uncultivated countryside", and believe me, this countryside was uncultivated and bleak. Majors Parker and Goldstein set up headquarters in some buildings along the road to Regne-Vielsalm. The balance of the troops defending this lonely piece of real estate came from remnants of other outfits that straggled by. Fortunately, some of the newcomers on our side had some fairly heavy armament, such as halftracks with multiple 50 calibers, assault 37-millimeters, tanks and the like. Eventually, Lieutenant Woodruff arrived with a platoon from the 82nd Airborne, and he had one or more 30-caliber machine guns on the corner with me. The fog was dense, so much so that we were not able to get any air support for lack of visibility, but at the same time this lack of observation worked to our advantage as I am sure the enemy was having trouble seeing us in order to lay down accurate fire.

John F. Gatens

Although historians have disagreed as to where the No. 1 howitzer was located, I can place it without question. My 105-mm. howitzer was at the intersection of the roads to Samree and Manhay, and laid in the direction of Regne; on the opposite corner and across the road from the farmhouse and barn.

On December 20, a tank from the Third Armored Division showed up. He parked in the road near the farmhouse, with his gun pointing down the road towards Manhay. Of course, we were very happy to see a tanker. One of the men jumped out and walked

134

up to the corner. He was looking in the direction of Regne. He wasn't there too long when he fell to the ground. A few of us went over to see what had happened to him. He had a bullet hole in his forehead. Unfortunately, he didn't have his helmet on, only the soft tanker's helmet that they wear. Needless to say, no one went wandering around after that. That's why I can't say where the other two howitzers were. I never did visit them, and I could not see them from my position. Immediately after the tanker fell, it was determined that he was hit by a sniper in the woods down the Regne Road. I was given an order (I can't remember by whom) to fire a few rounds into the trees. We never heard from anyone down there after that.

Arthur C. Brown

At one time, while I was moving around the position, a sergeant from another outfit and I were standing in the road and looking north toward Manhay. From the woods that came right down to the crossroads at the northwest point came the terrifying sound of a German machine pistol (burp gun). These guns were called "burp" because of the high cyclical rate of fire, sixteen hundred rounds per minute or so. The two of us dropped to the ground, and after the firing stopped, only I got up. My companion was dead with a bullet hole between the eyes. I ran over to the howitzer covering that sector and we swept the woods with tree top fire to clean out the snipers. As no more was heard from this area for awhile, the mission must have been successful.

John F. Gatens

Major Parker visited my position at least three times, always in good spirits and giving us encouragement. He would leave by saying, "Don't worry, we'll be leaving here pretty soon." Little did we know that he had ignored an order to displace to the north.

The most unusual fire mission that I received was from Major Parker. At that time I had no idea what he was doing, but I later learned that he had been advised that a large enemy force of armored and mechanized infantry was in position about four miles west of Samree along the Salmchateau road. Major Parker told me to turn my howitzer around approximately 180 degrees. We had to roll it forward until we had a good clearing in the trees. In the near distance there was a house. He gave me an elevation and then said, "I want you to come as close to the peak of that house as you can, without hitting it and we will fire." Looking through the sight I did that. I even looked through the tube to be sure, and asked my No. 1 man to verify that he couldn't see the house. I told Major Parker that I was ready, then he gave the order to fire. We fired four rounds. I don't know whether the other two sections also fired this mission. I can only state what my section did.

Elliott Goldstein

To complete the story of the unusual fire mission on Samree, we were aided by an officer from the 87th

Reconnaissance Troop of the 7th Armored Division. He had first observed the Germans in Samree and radioed the information back. The information was passed to Major Parker. The first round fired was reported by the observer to be range correct, deflection correct, and height of burst correct. Two or three volleys were then fired after which the observer reported, "Mission accomplished." Major Parker had used a 1/50,000 map to get the direction, a safety pin as a plotting pin and a house as the aiming point. He used a monkey wrench to set the fuses.

Randolph C. Pierson

It is cold, almost twenty degrees below freezing. The north wind is brisk. I am glad I got to spend the night in the security of the root cellar under the stone command post building. During the night, and early this morning, Major Parker had persuaded stragglers to stand and fight with us. They were: one light tank and crew from the 87th Recon Squadron; four 3-inch, high-velocity anti-tank guns and crews from the 643rd Tank Destroyer Battalion, and four anti-aircraft half-tracks from the 203rd AAA Battalion, three mounting Quad-Fiftys, one mounting a 37-mm. AA gun.

We received our first fire mission at approximately 1500 hours, "enemy infantry entering Samree, Belgium." This was strange since our defenses were facing east and north but Samree was to our northwest. We successfully completed the mission with the report, "Cease fire, enemy infantry withdrawing from Samree." We were confused and thought, "where in the HELL is the enemy? Another typical situation. No one knows anything, SNAFU!"

Our second activity occurred at about 2300 hours. Enemy infantry were reported approaching our positions from the east. The Quad-Fifty half-track covering that sector was alerted. They delivered devastating fire, which I watched from the road in front of the command post. It was beautiful and looked like four lines of giant fire flies chasing each other; however, I could not relate this beautiful sight to the carnage being created. A combat patrol was dispatched to "mop up" enemy survivors. The patrol found only one wounded German, many dead bodies, and scattered, mangled bicycles.

The main question was, what was this patrol doing? Why is it here? We could only guess. The wounded man died without speaking.

John F. Gatens

Captain Brown (another courageous man and a great leader) cautioned us that a group of Germans on bicycles were reported on the road leading to our position. He told us that when the order to fire was given, everyone should fire down that road. Boy, when those quad 50s opened up, so did we. The roar was deafening. The order was given to stop firing. Then all night you could hear men moaning in pain and calling for help. Even though I knew that they were the enemy, I couldn't help but feel sorry for them.

John R. Schaffner

I was sent forward to have a look around and found several dead German soldiers in the snow. I was not at all comfortable with that and was happy not to have found any live ones. The enemy had apparently pulled back after we had cut down their advance group the night before.

All that day was spent digging and improving our defensive perimeter. We were given some "warming time", off and on, inside the stone building being used as a command post. At one point I was detailed to guard two German prisoners that were brought in. I never learned the circumstances of their capture. One, an officer, spoke good English and warned us that the German Army was coming through us and would kill anyone in the way and push the rest into the English Channel, so we could save everybody a lot of trouble by surrendering to him right then and there.

At one point a Sherman tank came through our position, set up in front of our command post, and fired a few rounds across the field and into the forest in which some German soldiers were running from tree to tree for cover.

That night after an initial attack, I recall being in my foxhole waiting for the Germans to come at us again. The realization came to me that I was involved in a real risky business. The area was lighted by the flames of a pile of fuel drums burning throughout the rest of the night and reflecting eerily on the snow-covered ground. The only sounds were those made by the fire and the crying for help from the wounded enemy who were lying in the snow just out of view. I stayed in the foxhole all night and never did discover what finally happened to them; apparently their people abandoned them. Later I heard that one of our medics went out and checked on them and did what he could. Over the years I continue to feel some responsibility for their fate, since it was I who called for the fire on them when they first approached the crossroads. Responsible--yes; sorry--no. It was they or I.

A lot of things go through your mind when you think that it is your time to die, and I can clearly remember lying in that cold hole in the ground, that could shortly be my grave, thinking that I had not even experienced being "in love" yet. I definitely did not want to die in this strange place. I prayed to God, Jesus and every other deity that I could think of for help. In later years I heard the expression that "there were no atheists in foxholes." You can believe that.

Randolph C. Pierson

At 0530 hours, the first serious attack on our position began. About two platoons of enemy infantry in the forest east of the perimeter, supported by light mortar fire, seemed to be testing our defense capability. By daylight, howitzer and heavy automatic weapons fire had forced the enemy to withdraw. Only a single mortar continued to deliver interdiction fire into our position.

About 0800 hours, Major Parker dispatched the light reconnaissance tank to find and neutralize the mortar position. In a short time the tank returned to the

140

command post. The non-commissioned tank commander reported to the major that the mortar had been neutralized. He then produced five German "Soldier's Books" to identify the enemy unit attacking us and as proof of his kill.

This second fire fight proved to the enemy that we were there and planning to stay. So far, so good. No American casualties!

At 2000 hours Major Parker ordered me to man an observation post for the remainder of the night. He expected an enemy build-up during the night and needed a forward observer to adjust harassing fire. The walk to the observation post was dark and frightening. The observation post I manned was 800 or 900 yards east of our perimeter. I was alone except for my EEBA field telephone, my .45 caliber pistol, and my freshly-sharpened boot knife. I wished I was back at the command post.

CHAPTER XIV

The Battle Heats Up

Harold L. Kuizema

The Germans made their first attack in force early in the morning of the twenty-first. I fired my carbine from behind a truck, After the attack, in which many Germans were killed and wounded, we heard their calls of "Kamerad, Kamerad." One of the dead German soldiers lay approximately fifty feet from us. He was very young, perhaps a sixteen year-old. Major Parker ordered us to round up the German soldiers who had been taken prisoner. He asked me to accompany him with the prisoners as we directed them to the command post for interrogation.

Elliott Goldstein

My memories from the twenty-first onward are quite blurred. With the aid of the after action report, which I put together at Chateau Xhos, Belgium, I've tried to place what I remember in proper order. After we had organized our position for defense, Captains Brown and Huxel had the three howitzers covering the three principal roads, leaving the Manhay Road uncovered. Although our assignment was to protect the Division's supply route to Vielsalm, which presumably meant the road from the east running in a westerly direction, we assumed that an attack might come from the south or west as well as from the east. Our fields of fire were directed down the three roads. At shortly after midnight the southern outpost reported that a group of Germans on bicycles had stopped near his outpost and were examining the "daisy chain." The bicycle patrol was the first German group we encountered. (The incident is described earlier.)

While there was a certain euphoria in having repulsed the first attack, it was clear that the dead and wounded were part of a reinforced patrol and that others would soon follow them. During the remainder of the night, track vehicles were heard moving about, and there was some indication that enemy troops were in the area. We expected an attack. It came at about 0530 hours. Fortunately, we had a lot of firepower, and the attack was repulsed without casualties. I had alternated my position between the two houses being used as headquarters, and during the attack I would go outside and check on all the defensive positions. When the attack started, I moved into a position which commanded the road to the south and joined in the general firefight, which took place along that road. After two hours, the Germans withdrew. Six German dead were left in position, and fourteen prisoners were taken, six of them wounded. From interrogation it was learned that approximately eighty men from a Volksgrenadier outfit had attacked, led by a lieutenant from a Panzer Division. Their mission was to feel out the defenses.

From that point on we were under gradually increasing pressure. German snipers were active in the morning, and several were killed, although none was captured. At about 1200 hours a messenger from General McMahon brought orders for the battalion to withdraw to the vicinity of Brau for reorganization. The order was received from a messenger, rather than by radio, since our command radio was functioning only intermittently. At the time we went into our first position, our radios were supposedly calibrated. They were an early form of FM radio using crystals to set the frequencies. They were never properly calibrated, and we, for all practical purposes, had no communication with any command except through the radios of other outfits.

Not only did we have no communication; we had no orders and no assigned mission. General McMahon had, in effect, told us that our mission had been completed. We were under his command but had no communication with him. The outfits who came in to help us were under the command of 3rd Armored Division and 7th Armored Division, but we had no orders from either of them.

The 87th Reconnaissance Troop was ordered to hold the crossroads, but Major Parker did not want to leave until they had received reinforcements. Reinforcements did arrive in the form of two tank platoons. At about 1530 the Germans attacked from the east. We had not known that they had moved from the woods to the south around to the east, and they had approached within three hundred yards of our position before being detected. They had set up a roadblock about eight hundred yards east of us composed of wrecked American trucks. The fog was so heavy that we had not seen any of this. We opened fire with all of the armament we had available, and when two platoons of medium tanks from the Third Armored Division, Task Force Jones, rolled into our position, their additional fire power brought success to our defense. The tanks were supported by A Battery of the 54th Armored Field Artillery. Lieutenant Pratt of that battery was the forward observer. He and I went into the second story of one of the houses which we had been using for an observation post, but it was generally useless since we were not firing indirect fire. Lieutenant Pratt, who had more experience in this than we had, told us that we should throw out all the furniture on the second floor, knock out the windows and put mattresses and pillows against the walls below the windows for protection. It seemed a poor way to treat our Belgian host, but it was obviously the safest thing to do if the position were to be used as an observation post.

During the night a plan of fires was drawn up with Lieutenant Pratt's assistance. We also had added to our arsenal two 105-millimeter assault guns from Task Force Jones. It was reassuring to have them. To us our position seemed more like a way station than a defensive post, as reinforcements seemed to come and go. We did not know how long Task Force Jones was to stay with us, nor did we know whether we would get other reinforcements. We therefore pulled in our perimeter. All vehicles were moved inside the perimeter, and two-man emplacements were dug at five-yard intervals around a part of the perimeter. The perimeter was much smaller than it had been earlier since we'd suffered a number of casualties during the afternoon. Even with this reduced perimeter, we were only able to cover the east and south and had to rely on the anti-aircraft guns and the vehicles of the reconnaissance group to cover the remainder of the perimeter.

During the evening a squad from the 504th Parachute Infantry reported in. At about the same time we were informed by Task Force Jones that they had received orders to withdraw and that they would be relieved by a battalion of the 325th Glider Infantry. One company of glider infantry was to come in from the north at about 0300, and the remainder of the battalion was to enter the position from the east at daylight.

The parachute infantry squad was commanded by Staff Sergeant Wehner. I was impressed by the confidence of the paratroopers. They were completely professional, very "cool", and enjoyed the respect that we less experienced soldiers gave them. We suggested that they carry out two assignments. Sergeant Wehner was asked to detach two men and assign them to rendezvous with the company of the 325th Glider Infantry, which was to come in from the north, and lead them into position. The second assignment was to patrol the woods to the east and south and determine the German positions and their strength. This patrol reported back, after scouting the woods to the east, that the Germans were digging in. They did not patrol to the south. Authority was so multiple and divided that we could not give the paratroopers a direct order but could only make requests of them.

There was a heavy snowfall during the night, which added to our difficulties. All of us were in and out of the weather, but moisture soaked through shoes, and the freezing temperature increased the danger of trench foot. I was fortunate in that I had an extra pair of socks. Whenever I had a chance, I changed socks, and put the damp ones in my armpits under my clothes, which dried them out. This probably saved me from trench foot, and I had only slight damage to my hands and feet from freezing.

Calvin V. Abbott

When we set up at the crossroads, I went to the stone building we used as a command post. This was the first time I had seen Major Goldstein since we had left our second position. Some of us had foxholes at the back of the house. My recollection of days is not too accurate, since all the action runs into one continuous battle in my memory. I remember that three of us in a foxhole fired on the Germans every morning and night. We had a big piece of slate over the back of the foxhole that kept the shrapnel off of us. There was cold snow on the ground and slush in the foxhole. I had combat boots on, and they were wet and cold. One day after a battle with the Germans, I don't remember the time of day, Major Goldstein asked me to come with him. Major Goldstein had a forty-five pistol, and I had my carbine as we walked to the back of a house where we had directed our fire. Major Goldstein jumped over a ditch and shouted something that I didn't understand. Several Germans stood up. One of them had his arm blown off at the elbow and was bleeding profusely. We marched them back to the command post where a medic treated the Germans, and all were sent back to our rear echelon as prisoners of war.

Later, I believe on the same day, a man and a woman came out of the woods where the Germans were. We stopped them. They said they wanted to see whoever was in charge. A soldier ran and got Major Goldstein. The man and woman said they lived in the house and wanted to come back. The Major said it wasn't safe for them and they couldn't come in; so they went back from whence they came.

Another time the three of us were in our foxhole. It was getting near daylight. I looked out. In front of our hole was a German with his hands at the edge of the foxhole--dead. One of us had shot him during the night. He had dynamite with him, which I believe he had intended to either throw or plant at the house we were using as a command post.

John R. Schaffner

Very early, while still dark on the morning of December 22, the Germans attacked again, and we were subjected to small arms and mortar fire off and on all day. At one point, mortar rounds were landing real close to my foxhole, and I was feeling very exposed with no helmet to crawl into. I could hear the mortar fragments and bullets smacking into the ground just outside my hole. Most of the mortar rounds were falling farther in toward the buildings. I saw one hit the roof of Captain Brown's command post. It must have been during this time that Major Parker was wounded by a fragment. I'm not sure about that; I didn't witness it. There was a GI in a foxhole next to mine who would not fire his weapon. When I called on him to fire, he just looked at me. I didn't know him and don't know his ultimate fate. I could not understand why he was not willing to help himself (and the rest of us). I have read since that this is not an unusual occurrence. There are always a certain number who will not squeeze that trigger, even when their life is threatened.

Late in the afternoon several tanks were heard approaching our position. Thankfully, they were ours. They rolled out in the open and fired their big guns into the German positions, and I thought, no problem now. With all this help, the day is saved. It got quiet again, and then the tanks left. Looked like we would be hung out to dry, but it did stop the enemy attack for a while. Thanks, tankers. Too bad you couldn't stay for dinner.

After dark I was moved in closer to the command post and dug another hole along with a GI named Randy Pierson. One of our guys made a run from hole to hole tossing everybody something to eat. I caught a box of "wet-or-dry" cereal and ate it dry. The two of us spent the night in the hole. One of us would sleep an hour and the other keep watch and then we would alternate. This was the only kind of rest that anybody got. We had dug our hole reasonably deep and then further fortified it with some fence rails that we criss-crossed in front of it. I was sure that we would be attacked that night. I had thirty rounds of carbine ammunition remaining and a knife that I placed on the ground where I could reach it. I prayed that this would not be necessary. It got very cold that night, and the enemy did not attack. Another very long night.

At this time the weather was our worst enemy; but then in the morning things changed and the weather was reduced to second place.

Elliott Goldstein

I had been outside during the night and concluded that the Germans were preparing to attack before daybreak. We heard vehicles moving and were aware of movements of infantry. We decided that rather than waiting for the Germans to attack, we would make a preemptive strike, simulating a counterattack by our forces. We commenced firing at 0530. Between the indirect fire of the armored field artillery, the direct fire of our three howitzers and the fire of the 50-caliber machine guns, it sounded like a full-scale battle.

Again, our lack of communication could have resulted in disaster. A company from the 325th Glider Infantry, which was approaching from the north as reinforcements, heard the sound of firing and very properly deployed in a defensive position about two hundred yards north of the crossroads. At about 0800 the tanks and Lieutenant Pratt, the forward observer for the armored field artillery, left as directed by their orders of the night before. At about 1200 the company of the 325th Glider Infantry finally arrived, guided in by scouts from the 504th Parachute Infantry. We did not know it at the time, but the remainder of the battalion went into position on the high ground to the east, overlooking the crossroads near the village of Fraiture. A platoon of the glider infantry went forward, after briefing, to dig in on the line of resistance held by the 589th.

The plan of the 325th Glider Infantry company was to have one platoon relieve the men from the 589th on the perimeter and to hold the remainder of the company in reserve. When the platoon went forward to dig in, they were met by a heavy mortar barrage, and were forced to retreat. They incurred about fifteen casualties who were evacuated. While the glider infantry was reorganizing, the 589th and those who had joined it continued to man the outposts on the perimeter.

As we had learned to our sorrow, an artillery battery on the road is a particularly vulnerable target, easy to hit and particularly defenseless. To withdraw, we had to have protection for the crews to get the howitzers out of their dug-in positions and hitched to the prime movers. The remainder of the personnel could follow, after covering the retreat of the howitzer crews. To effect this, we had to have troops of sufficient strength to cover our withdrawal. Since the infantry was not holding the perimeter, the 589th could not leave until the infantry had reorganized and taken their assigned positions. This was not completed until after dark, so the 589th personnel remained in position.

To coordinate the perimeter, I thought it was important that I be outside with the defenders whenever there was a firefight. Conditions were severe since we had to contend not only with the enemy, but with the cold and snow. However, the snow helped us since it forced the Germans to use the roads, and with our heavy firepower covering the roads, we were able to hold them, if not at bay, at least outside the perimeter.

Additional firepower was made available to the defenders by the support of A Battery of the 54th Armored Field Artillery Battalion. At about 1400 a scout sergeant from that battery reported to the company commander of the glider infantry that the battery would support his troops. Several concentrations were fired, but since visibility was poor, it was difficult to observe the fire or to determine its effect. Incoming mortar fire continued from the woods.

I cannot explain today why Major Parker and I gathered with commanders of the other troops inside the perimeter on a road in full view of the Germans. I believe that Major Parker was laying out a field order which would result in the commander of the glider infantry taking over the defense of the position. Before he could say anything, the Germans dropped a mortar shell into the middle of our group. I was knocked backwards and was hit by several shell fragments. Although one penetrated to the skin, I had enough layers of clothing so that I was not wounded. Major Parker was not so fortunate, and since the explosion was closest to him, he was severely wounded and was evacuated, and I took over command.

During the night the Germans infiltrated into the woods to the north and established a line of troops at the edge of the woods all of the way down to the Vielsalm Road.

John C. Rain

I was with a group, which included Bernard Strohmier, who were in foxholes at the crossroads. One night when mortar fire was heavy, we were told to fall back to the rock barn for protection. The word didn't reach Strohmier, so that when we went back in the morning, there he was in his hole. He'd been there all alone the entire night. His first words were "Got my German." The corpse was laying out in front of him. I think he made them think that we were still there. He should have been decorated for his courage.

Barney M. Alford Jr.

From the beginning to the end of the fighting at the crossroads, I was with my gun crew. My gun was in position covering the road to Houffalize. I participated in every firefight of the entire period. I can confirm everything that has been said about those days. Our orders were to fire down the road at any enemy who appeared, and we did. We had periods of quiet followed by periods of intense action. We were involved in every one of many firefights.

Harold J. Kuizema

The fog, cold, and snow continued on December 22, and from early on, we were busy trying to dig our

154

foxholes as deep as we could. We dug them around the house. The weather conditions made digging, as it did everything else, very difficult. There were two of us in each foxhole, and we lived there with an army blanket. Sadly, I don't remember the name of the man I shared my foxhole with. We were mainly concerned with surviving. One was always on guard, so it was not a very social time. Keeping alert was crucial to survival. The feeling was one of constant fear.

We were kept busy, with an attack in the morning and another in the afternoon. The truck just behind us, a half-track mounting a machine gun, intermittently sprayed the area in front of us to flush out snipers.

Prior to my army experience, my belief in God was firmly established. I can't say that I thought about it a great deal in the service. Fulfilling our duties, keeping warm, and just surviving were our priorities. I know that the prayers of my family and my church followed me.

Bernard C. Strohmier

I was assigned to B Battery as a light truck driver and lineman in the wire section. Since the 15th Field Artillery Battalion (of the 2nd Infantry Division) had left its communication equipment in place, I never functioned as a lineman. During the first engagement, I functioned as a rifleman. When we displaced from our second position, I was fortunate enough to be in a truck which managed to get through Schönberg, and I reached Parker's Crossroads with the others who fought there.

155

At the crossroads, I spent most of my time dug in on the perimeter covering the approach from the highway leading to Houffalize. Frank Beaver, the battery switchboard operator, and John Rain, who was Captain Brown's radio operator, shared a foxhole on the same perimeter. Kenneth Sewell, also a light truck driver and lineman, was the man who set up the telephone line to this part of the perimeter and who spread the land mines on the road to Houffalize. He was the man who reported the German soldiers' arrival at the location of the land mines. His report to Captain Brown resulted in direct fire on the Germans. It was an experience I'll never forget, hearing the AAA people firing their quad 50-caliber machine guns and 37-mm. cannon from behind me over my position. And seeing and hearing the riflemen firing down the road on the Germans. All this firepower was effective in repelling the patrol. Our group on the perimeter had no casualties, but one went into shock. During one of the firefights, Frank Beaver became unresponsive and was unable to function, so John Rain had to man their position by himself. (Frank spent the rest of his life in a veteran's hospital.)

Randolph C. Pierson

During the early evening, probably about 1730 hours, one of the anti-aircraft half-tracks, assisting in the defense of Baraque de Fraiture, received a direct hit from a German round. I suspect it was a large caliber mortar round, but of course I don't actually know what type of munition it was. The results of this direct hit were swift and severe. From the command post we could hear the wounded men of the anti-aircraft crew screaming for help and also hear their 50-caliber ammunition starting to explode. This sight in the dark of night was dazzling, but grisly dazzling-- including vision of the half-track slowly becoming engulfed with flames fed by its gasoline and motor oil, and of the spectacular flight of exploding 50-caliber incendiary rounds as they arched high into the cold winter sky.

I was stationed just outside the command post building, trying to make up my mind what I should do. Move to the half-track and try to assist the wounded men stationed there, or remain at my assigned post? The front door of the command post burst open while I was debating with myself, and Technical Sergeant Frank Tacker, the Battalion Intelligence Noncommissioned Officer, ran past me in the dark shouting for someone to help him assist the wounded men in the half-track.

My doubts now gone, I followed Sergeant Tacker into the night toward the burning half-track and its exploding ammunition. Frank Tacker reached the burning vehicle moments before I arrived, and with one powerful leap, cleared the armored side of the vehicle and landed feet first in the fighting compartment. In one fluid motion he lifted one wounded GI over the side of the half-track and dropped him into my outstretched arms. I barely had time to lower the body on his back in the snow when the second body came over the armored side of the half-track, quickly followed by Sergeant Tacker

157

himself. At this point my heart was pounding and my breathing labored. I was terrified. Of course, I cannot speak for Frank. Outwardly he was calm as we checked the two men for wounds. It did not take a medical doctor to determine that one man was dead and the other badly injured.

I helped Technical Sergeant Tacker place the badly wounded man on his shoulders, and he started carrying this man on the long, slippery, and dangerous trek back to the command post and to a waiting medic. As I tried to drag the dead GI body away from the fury of the burning vehicle and the exploding ammunition, the badly burned flesh of the man's wrists and forearms came off on my woolen gloves. I quit dragging the body, moved away from the burning vehicle, leaned over in the darkness, and retched in the snow. The terrible sight and horrible smell caused by the burned flesh was too much for my stomach.

How my friend Frank Tacker managed to carry the heavy weight of the wounded man back to the command post through the ice and snow, and in the darkness, is beyond me. Frank was a young man with considerable physical strength, a deep sense of responsibility, immense personal courage, and strong moral character. Time has probably diminished Frank's physical strength; however, nothing will ever diminish his other sterling qualities or the undying respect I have for him as a man.

Fiction writers would give this incident a happy Hollywood ending. History does not. The severely wounded man died on Frank's shoulders before they reached the command post. Frank returned to his job of collecting intelligence information. I returned to my assigned post outside the command post, smoked a cigarette in cupped hands, and as I smoked, I trembled from the realization that Frank and I had barely escaped serious injury or possible death.

This incident was only one of many such incidents which occurred during the intense fury of the battle for Parker's Crossroads as it continued unabated. During this battle no quarter was asked by the 589th, and no quarter was given!

Elliott Goldstein

We fell into a pattern of repelling an attack, and then a period of quiet. Everyone was under a strain, since we knew that after an attack was repelled we could expect another attack soon thereafter. Each time an attack started you could hear the sound of urine hitting the snow as the "fight or flight" syndrome kicked in. In this case, the result was always "fight"-- not "flight".

During the night of December 22, I realized the awful responsibility that a commander has in combat. We repelled an attack, and a soldier who was manning a 50-caliber machine gun on an anti-aircraft mount was severely wounded. I went to him to take him to the aid station, and he said, 'Major, I stayed here and kept firing like you said." He was only one of many who were critically wounded following orders in holding our position.

C H A P T E R   XV

The Battle Finally Ends

Calvin V. Abbott

During the night of December 22, I went into the house to get coffee and warm up. The door opened, and in walked a German officer and a German soldier with a white flag, escorted by some of our men. Major Goldstein told us to take them upstairs and tie their hands behind them, which we did. The Germans wanted a cigarette, and we put one in each of their mouths and lit it. They told us that the Germans would attack the next day with tanks and infantry and we should give up. But we didn't. The next day Major Goldstein ordered us to put our captives in the back of a truck, and the Major asked me if I wanted to ride shotgun on the truck, but I declined. There was but one road out (the road in front of the house), and everyone seemed to agree that the truck would not make it.

John R. Schaffner

It seems that each time our perimeter got smaller the Germans got closer, and appeared ready to end it. The fog would roll in and out giving us limited visibility. I would fire at anything I saw moving around in range of my foxhole. The weather was tough on us, but I think it was to our advantage from a defensive point of view. I'm sure our enemy was not

161

able to determine exactly what he had to overcome to take the crossroads. Whenever he came into view, we would drive him back into the fog. Our ammunition was running out. I had one clip of carbine rounds and could find no more. Word had come around that when the ammo ran out and the Germans came, it would be every man for himself to escape if he could; otherwise, a surrender was prudent. We were apparently surrounded, but the Germans were taking the easiest route, the hard surface roads. That left the fields open.

Late afternoon on December 23, probably at about 1600, the final assault came. Mortars, small arms and fire from tanks. I was in the stone building sitting on the floor with my back to the wall. Harold Kuizema was with me. This room must have been a kitchen at one time because I recall a wood burning cook stove and a GI whom I didn't know trying to heat something on it. Something big hit that wall and exploded right over our heads into the room. It must have hit high or it would have gotten both of us. As it was, it filled the room with debris and dust. That was all the motivation we needed to leave. To wait for another one never crossed my mind. We (Harold and I) went to the front door. They were coming in and we were going out. It was that simple. Some of our people were going to the cellar. I didn't like that idea. So once outside we crawled to the road and into the ditch. There were some cattle milling about on the road and much smoke, so we got up and ran through the cattle to the ditch on the far side and once again dropped down below ground level to avoid the German fire. On this side of the road was a snow-covered field very open, but it was "away" from the attack so that's the direction we took. Not far into the field Harold went down. As I got to him I saw two GIs approaching from the other direction. It was apparent that Harold was not going any farther on his own so between the three of us we moved him the remaining distance to the shelter of the woods and into the company of a patrol of infantrymen from the 82nd Airborne Division.

When we reached the shelter of the woods and I looked back at the crossroads, the whole sky seemed to be lighted by the flames from the burning building and vehicles. Our wounded Harold was evacuated, and I received permission to tag along with these 82nd Airborne Division GIs, which I did until late sometime the next day (December 24) when I was able to locate some 106th Division people. I was beginning to feel at home.

Randolph C. Pierson

The first round of the predawn German artillery preparation landed at 0430 hours. It was from a German 88-mm. The enemy had moved artillery within range of the crossroads. We had no capability to return fire. We could only hunker down, curse, and wait for the inevitable. Automatic arms fire was coming from the north and south flanks of the perimeter for the first time. The German infantry had moved through the forest in an effort to flank us. This forced a corresponding change in our defense lines and weapons emplacements. This turned out to be a determined attack. It lasted until about 0945 hours, almost five hours. Five hours under direct fire is an eternity in close combat!

We took casualties, both KIAs and WIAs. Why did we continue to fight? Why did the guys in the other units continue to make war? They were getting killed too! It didn't make sense! Its like everyone had a death wish. We all knew what the outcome would be, yet we didn't quit!

At 1600 hours the third attack of the day started. The artillery preparation was more vicious and gut wrenching than before. This experience is impossible for me to describe. It affects people differently. Some break and run, only to be cut down by shell fragments or small arms fire. Others, like me, dig in and mentally try to block out the inevitable and the mayhem which surrounds us.

Advance elements of the 2nd and 9th SS Panzer Divisions were using armor to exert tremendous pressure on our defenses from both the south and east. Our heavy weapons were their prime targets. They are losing Panzers, but we are losing the battle of attrition.

Elliott Goldstein

At about 0430 an SS patrol attacked from the southeast at the same time as an attack was made by the Germans on the northeast of the perimeter. Both attacks were repulsed, and an SS officer and sergeant were captured. Interrogation disclosed that they were from the 2nd SS Panzer Division.

During the morning, the Germans continued the mortar and heavy weapons fire. We found that a platoon of towed tank destroyers from the 643rd Tank Destroyer Battalion had set up during the night outside our perimeter and had been surrounded by the Germans and captured at about 0900. The Germans set up the captured guns to fire on us. Fortunately, we had the support of the assault guns, which fired into the Germans north of us. Two of our mortar crews were knocked out and one rocket gun was destroyed.

A Battery of the 54th Armored Field Artillery had been adjusted during the night on German mortar crews which had moved out into the open. After daylight the crews moved back into the woods where observation became difficult. Communication also became difficult since the Germans had captured radios on the artillery's frequency and intercepted all our commands.

At about 1000 hours a company from the 509th Parachute Infantry Battalion moved in from the north, freed the captured tank destroyers and then prepared to attack to the west.

The German artillery and mortar fire had cut all telephone lines, so new lines were laid to all command posts. However, no wire was laid to the howitzers or the 50-caliber machine guns, so Captains Brown and Huxel, and Lieutenant Wright went to each gun and howitzer to order fire missions. This morning Captain Huxel was injured by a mortar fragment but refused to be evacuated. After he was injured, Captain Brown and Lieutenant Wright went to the guns in full view of the Germans, and adjusted A Battery of the 5th Armored F.A. Battalion on German soldiers attempting to infiltrate our positions.

I ordered all outposts to be pulled in, in order to permit the armored vehicles to maneuver, and plans were made to repel an attack that, according to the prisoners, was planned for that night. I knew that we needed more reinforcements than had been sent to us and that our only chance to get everyone out was to have sufficient reinforcements to permit us to withdraw.

I was told by one of the armored force officers that Lieutenant Colonel Walter P. Richardson, commanding Task Force Y of the 3rd Armored Division under General Rose, was in charge of the defense in our area. If we were to get reinforcements, he was the man I had to see. I took the two SS prisoners with me and drove to Manhay. When I arrived at Manhay, I saw Colonel Richardson almost immediately. He knew we needed help when he saw the two SS prisoners. While we did not have access to any intelligence, he had communications from his Division G2 and knew what we didn't know--that there was a major attack coming our way and that it was tactically important to hold the crossroads.

He ordered Major Olin F. Brewster to accompany me back to the crossroads so that he could take command of the defense. He ordered a platoon each of armored infantry and of medium tanks and a company of paratroopers from the 509th Parachute Infantry Regiment to go to the crossroads immediately. The company of the 509th was able to get to the crossroads prior to the German attack. The other units were held up by a German roadblock. [I was so shocked by the catastrophes which followed that my memory of the

166

sequence of events was cloudy, but Major (now Lieutenant Colonel) Brewster's recollections set out below aided my memory.] We drove towards the crossroads from Manhay. We were stopped before we got to the crossroads by troops who said we couldn't proceed down the road. Major Brewster and I parked the jeeps and walked towards the crossroads. My memory is very vivid, however, of a round, fired by a tank, going by us in the center of the road. It looked as though it was only six feet off the ground, and flying in a flat trajectory. It was close, so we wasted no time taking to the woods and tried to reach the crossroads through them. We were never able to get close, and meanwhile, artillery shells were bursting in the treetops and showering shell fragments throughout the area. We finally concluded that we couldn't go farther and retreated. It was the saddest day of my life. I had accomplished my mission, but too late to see it through, and I felt that I had let down the brave men who had fought so valiantly, and whom I'd left behind.

The principal emotion I felt was anger, anger at myself for not succeeding in extricating my command from the trap; anger at the Germans; anger at the commander, whoever he might be, for not having sooner sent aid to us. Although I had escaped almost certain capture or death, I felt neither happy nor relieved since the men I commanded were being overrun. I thought all our efforts had come to naught.

Olin F. Brewster

Colonel Richardson directed me to report to him in Manhay after noon on December 23. He introduced me to Major Elliott Goldstein, and the major explained the grave situation they were in. The colonel sent Goldstein and me back to the crossroads to see what we could do to help. The major and I were stopped about a half mile from the crossroads and told not to go farther in our jeeps because the crossroads had been overrun and the Germans were occupying it. We dismounted and moved out through the woods on the left of the road trying to get a better view. These woods were pretty dense and sight distance very limited. We got a few hundred yards from our objective when a German tank took us under fire with a 75-mm. gun. We returned to our jeeps, and I radioed the situation to the colonel. There was nothing left to defend with. He had me return to Manhay and he ordered a medium tank company and an infantry company that were in the Erezee area to move to Manhay.

When I arrived back at Manhay, it was about dark. There I met Captain Cobb, Commander of H Company, 332nd Infantry Regiment, and Captain Siegel, Commander of Company A of a separate battalion of the 509th Parachute Infantry Regiment. I had never heard of the 509th before, but found out that they made combat jumps from North Africa to Europe. Colonel Richardson's orders were brief, "Retake the crossroads." It was cold, dark, and snow was on the ground when we moved out. Company H had six M-4 tanks and the infantry company had approximately 150 men. The tanks moved out on the road, and the infantry moved out on foot on each shoulder of the road. Things went well for the first few miles, but just as the lead tank reached crossroad 545-875 (Belle-Haie), it was fired on and hit by an enemy tank in the vicinity of Parker's Crossroads. Because of the terrain and woods, we were unable to move our tanks any farther south, so I chose to go into a defensive position in the area of Belle-Haie.

Harold J. Kuizema

Today the shelling became very close and intense. The morning attack was severe, and the afternoon attack was even more intense. That afternoon a piece of shrapnel hit my thumb while I was in my foxhole. The wound was jagged and bleeding but was minor compared to what I saw next at the first-aid station located in the house used as a command post. There I saw men with faces blown off and others pulling teeth out of their mouths. I also saw a German prisoner being interrogated by one of our officers, using one of our soldiers as an interpreter.

While I was in the command post, a group from the 82nd Airborne joined the defense. They had come on foot and their eagerness to join in the battle impressed me. "Where are the bazookas?", they asked. They were gung ho to get into action. It came sooner than they thought--there was a direct hit on the house. A fire started. I ran out of the house, crawling on my stomach under a fence when the explosion of a shell nearby wounded me in the left leg. My leg was numb, but I tried to crawl away, realizing I needed help. A medic nearby bound my wound, using my first-aid kit. John Schaffner came to my aid, and with his help, I got to the aid station of some 82nd Airborne troops. From there it was by jeep, with other wounded, to a field hospital, and after a few days I was moved to other hospitals, and finally I was moved to a hospital in England in which I was treated for my wound and a bad case of frozen feet.

Calvin V. Abbott

Early on the next day (December 23), the Germans hit with mortar fire. We were in our foxhole; one shell hit in front and the next to the left. We jumped out and ran to the rock house. The tanks were coming across the field, firing and hitting the house, catching it on fire. There were cows and chickens in the barn built onto the house. We ran them out through the big barn door. In between the room and barn, there was a little room with an iron wash pot. The tanks got closer and closer, firing on the house. I got behind the wash pot thinking that would stop a shell. While I was lying behind it, about four feet above my head there was a big bang and then a big hole appeared in the wall. Someone gave the order to destroy our weapons and we did. Someone tried to stick a white handkerchief out the window. The Germans shot it down. Someone ran to the door on one side and there was a tank with an 88 muzzle right in his face. We put our hands up and walked out. The soldiers in behind the tanks started firing at us so we hit the ground. This went on two or three times. I was lying beside a tank when the hatch opened and a German officer raised his hand to cease fire. He told us (in English) that we had put up a good fight.

The German soldiers marched us out to the road and took our cigarettes. Someone said they were SS soldiers. They then took us to the ditch and told us to get on our knees with hands behind our heads. We did. Some Germans got out in front of us with burp guns ready to fire on us. You could hear our men praying out loud. I was too. We thought we were goners, but American artillery started coming in. We all started running. We and the Germans ran into the woods. We couldn't escape because there were Germans all around us. After the firing ceased, they gathered us up and marched us down the road.

For ninety-seven or ninety-eight days I was a prisoner of war.

Bernard C. Strohmier

I had little, if any, knowledge as to what was going on at the crossroads since I spent most of my time on the perimeter. I had all I could do to be a part of the defense against every attack. When I finally got word to come back to the stone house, it was on fire, and soon after that we were taken prisoner on the afternoon of December 23. We were taken to the other side of the road and lined up on the road to Houffalize. We noticed that a German officer, probably one Horst Gresiak, left his small car, an off-white or sand-

171

colored vehicle, in front of us. A German tank came up the road, ran over it and crushed it like a tin can. Surprisingly, the officer didn't protest--only ordered us to toss the wreck into a ditch by the road.

Barney M. Alford Jr.

When it became apparent that we were going to be overrun by the enemy, Captain Brown came by my gun and told us that we were on our own, but to hold on as long as we could. We did stay and hold our position for quite some time, but it soon became time for us to leave, or be captured or killed. I urged my gun crew to follow me and some of them did.

The enemy was firing smoke shells, or something that created smoke, which, when mixed with the fog, provided good cover. By taking advantage of it, and using all other available protective cover, such as farm sheds, disabled equipment, and ditches along roads, I was able to cross two roads and enter the forest. Here the trees and underbrush provided concealment that permitted us to move freely.

The men who were following me decided on our way to take cover in a building we passed, but I continued on. After carefully making my way through the forest, and some open areas, I met some GIs who knew where the 82nd Airborne Division lines were, and with their help, I entered their lines, which meant safety and food. What happened after that as I continued the war, is another story.

Randolph C. Pierson

The situation was impossible. We were pinned down and chewed up. Captain George Huxel advised the few remaining Headquarters Battery men that they had more than fulfilled their mission. It was decision time and we were on our own.

This information triggered much discussion among the eight or nine GIs in the shelter of the cellar. There was no consensus of opinion. Some wanted to try to escape, some elected to stay and take their chances, and some were undecided. The top floor of the building was smoldering. I did not relish life as a prisoner of war, and I certainly was not going to hunker down in a dark cellar and wait for someone to roll a grenade down the stairs. I pulled on my overcoat, strapped on my web belt, grabbed a carbine, went to the front door of the command post and waited.

The distance from the command post building to the edge of the forest appeared to be about the length of four football fields; however, I had to negotiate two ice-encrusted drainage ditches, climb over three low fences, contend with a roughly plowed, snow-covered field, and all the time encumbered with heavy winter clothing and overshoes, in a dark olive-drab uniform that stood out against the stark white snow like a sore thumb, while under direct observation of God only knows how many heavily armed German SS troops. I figured out I had two chances of making the trip alive. Slim and none!

The trip across the open ground was a nightmare come to life. Red and yellow tracers crossed my path.

Small arms fire nipped at my body, ripping holes in my outer clothing and kicking chunks of ice and snow onto my face. About halfway to the tree line, I slipped and fell. As I lay there, winded, I could see another person leave the command post building, only to be skewered by angry tracers as he tried to negotiate the second fence. I lay there, amazingly detached, as I saw more tracers tear into his already dead body as it dangled on the fence. Suddenly a white phosphorous round exploded nearby and I was surrounded by white smoke and struck by angry, flesh-searing particles of phosphorous.

With the aid of my sheath knife, I frantically tore away burning pieces of cloth and gouged holes in my exposed flesh in an effort to rid myself of the tormenting hot phosphorous. Without thinking, I rose and started running again in a semi-crouch toward the distant trees. With no idea of what awaited me in that tree line, I continued to crouch and run.

Both wounded and winded, I finally reached cover in the dense Ardennes Forest. Hidden behind a large evergreen, I stopped momentarily to catch my breath and get my bearings. I then turned in the direction I thought was north. Limping from the pain and struggling against the deep snow, I fought my way through the forest toward Manhay and never once looked back at the carnage in Baraque de Fraiture.

John F. Gatens

Captain Brown gave me permission to let the members of the section go across the street, a few at a time, to the farmhouse to get out of the weather and maybe warm up a little. But he ordered that at no time should the section be unable to complete a fire mission.

Around mid-afternoon on December 23 we started to receive an artillery barrage. It was light at first, then started to get heavier. Captain Brown had warned us that after the shelling stopped, we might be attacked by German infantry, so we should be ready. With that in mind, I ran across the street to get my men back to our position. Before we got out the door, the shelling was all around us and very heavy. The house was hit and burning. The concussion from all of the bursts blew me back into a wall. I sat there and felt my body all the way down to my legs to make sure that everything was still here.

Immediately after the shelling stopped, the German infantry were all around the house and a German tank was at the door. A German officer ordered us out and told us that if we were not out of the house immediately, he would order the tank to fire into the house. That was the end of the war for me as the great stand at Parker's Crossroads collapsed. For the next four months I was a prisoner of war.

Frank Tacker (as told to Randolph C. Pierson)

Everyone knew we could not hold out any longer. We had lost our firepower and most of our men. We were low on food and ammunition. We could no longer stop the huge German concentration of infantry and armor attacking us. However, the word from the captain that each man was on his own came as a total surprise to me. There were several men in the command post building when we received this news. Technician Fourth Grade Randy Pierson was one of those men.

Randy made up his mind very quickly, arguing he was not going to sit in a damned dark cellar and wait for some Kraut to throw a hand grenade down the stairs. He wanted to try to get to the lines of the 82nd Airborne Division, which we suspected were in the area of Manhay. The decision was easier for Randy than it was for me; he was not the senior noncommissioned officer in the group and had no real command function, as he was a technician. I was the senior noncom present and had a responsibility to the group.

At this point, no solution to our problem was clear. I watched some of the men try, unsuccessfully, to escape across the open ground between the command post and the tree line. Randy made it. He was lucky. I saw other men try and saw them die. When I told the remaining few what I had seen, there were those who chose to remain under cover rather than attempt to leave. Of course, their decision to stay meant I had to remain also.

There was one more compelling reason I chose to stay at the crossroads. It seems naive in retrospect, but I fully expected American troops to come and get us out.

The details of our existence during the last night are not clear. Why we were not detected is beyond me. Several times during the night, German troops walked through the rubble of the building which hid the entrance to the cellar in which we hid. There was one member of our little group who lost control and had to be physically restrained and gagged every time we heard someone walking on the floor above our heads. He was an older man, I did not know him; I think he was a cook.

The morning of December 24 broke clear and the crossroads were bombed by the RAF. This was an unnerving experience, as we sustained near misses, and with each exploding bomb, dirt and pieces of the cellar ceiling broke loose and fell on our heads.

After the bombing there was an extended period of complete silence. I lost track of time, but eventually we decided the Germans had moved on and felt it was time to exit the cellar and decide what to do. With great difficulty we raised the cellar door and moved from almost total darkness into bright sunlight which reflected off the white snow. For a moment, we were all blinded. When my vision returned to normal, I saw that we were in the center of what appeared to be the bivouac area for a battalion-sized German unit.

I turned to tell the other members of the group to get back in the cellar, but it was too late. We were looking squarely into the muzzles of burp guns held by SS troopers. The end of our experience was simple and quick. We dropped our weapons, raised our hands, and one German trooper said calmly in perfect English, "You are our prisoners. You will follow me!"

This is the way combat ended for me. I spent the rest of the war as a prisoner of war in Germany.

Robert C. Ringer

During the battle at Baraque de Fraiture, I commanded the Ammunition Train of the 591st Field Artillery. From the eleventh of December until the twenty-first of December, I led ammunition trains south to a depot at Bourcy (near Bastogne) and north to depots at Vervieres, and at Sprimont, both of which were in the vicinity of Liege. Our travels up and down Highway N15 took us through Parker's Crossroads many times.

On the 19th or 20th, I was requested by Lieutenant Colonel Phillip Hoover, who commanded the 591st Field Artillery Battalion, to take Lieutenant Thomas Wright and an enlisted man, whose name I don't remember, to the Crossroads. Since I had a three-quarter ton truck, my driver and I were able to take them there. Little did any of us know what they were getting into.

After March 15, 1945, I was given command of Service Battery of the 590th Field Artillery. There I learned that eleven men from that battery had been at the Crossroads. Only two escaped. One, Corporal Horace Duke, emerged shell-shocked. The other, Sergeant John Wagoner, had managed to escape with Captain Huxel. I didn't know, nor was I able to find out what happened to the others. So I was unable to be of any help to the distraught families who wrote to me for news of their sons.

Elliott Goldstein

So ended the defense of Parker's Crossroads! Was it worth the cost? It depends upon your point of view, but in retrospect it was one of the essential factors in limiting the Bulge and reversing Hitler's last offensive. In warfare on the scale of the Battle of the Bulge, the generals see only the big picture--the movement of companies, battalions, regiments, divisions and corps. From their viewpoint, the defense anchored by the men of the 589th was crucial to halting the "blitzkrieg" by which the German High Command planned to go through Belgium, flank the American armies, and cut off their main supply route. Like the defense of Bastogne and of St. Vith, the defense of Baraque de Fraiture delayed the advance of more than one German division. Unlike the defenses of those two towns, which were of division strength, under the command of a general, the crossroads were defended only by the remnants of a field artillery battalion, in conjunction with small units of infantry, parachute infantry, and armor--and without overall command. Their defense was a glorious chapter in the larger battle, an action which gave Major General James M. Gavin, commanding general of the 82nd Airborne Division, the time he needed to marshal his forces and stop the German advance along Highway N-15 through Manhay to Liege. To General Gavin, as quoted from a letter to Major Parker, "That stand your defenders made at the crossroads was one of the greatest actions of the war."

To the enlisted men and officers of the 589th who knew nothing of the big picture, the small picture showed a life-and-death struggle, precipitated by a decision of their commanders to stand and fight. The courage and determination of everyone involved resulted in a small force holding a defensive position until they were overrun by massive enemy forces, and the defense destroyed by weight of arms. At that time a survivor might have felt that the loss of the dead and wounded, and the capture of many, who suffered captivity for many months, was too high a price to pay for the defense of an obscure crossroads. But when the big picture became known, it was clear that the sacrifices made by the defenders were not only in the noblest traditions of the United States Army. Their stand, which materially delayed the German advance, saved the lives of thousands of American troops and helped to protect the civilians in Belgium from the advancing German army.

All officers, from generals to small unit commanders, bear the burden of their knowledge that each decision they make affects the lives not only of members of their commands, but of many other commands and the populace; and all affected are fellow human beings who put their lives and futures in the hands of their soldiers.

Those who have been in combat have an experience that they cannot easily describe. At this distance from 1944, there is a certain glamour attached to the defense of Parker's Crossroads, and deservedly so. However, to those who fought there, it was a brutal, filthy, and exhausting business in which the odds were finally overwhelmingly against them. We hope that you, the reader, will now have a better idea of why those who have been there say, "War is Hell!", and will understand why I am so proud of the brave men who fought to the end (and to many, their end) with such courage and determination.

SS-Obersturmfuehrer Horst Gresiak was the commander of the II Battalion, Second SS Panzer Regiment, the unit which overran the defense at Baraque de Fraiture. Obersturmfuehrer Gresiak was a veteran of many battles on the Russian front. After the war ended, he was interrogated by Allied personnel. This was his description of the Battle of Parker's Crossroads:

"Although brief, it was the most violent and the toughest battle that I experienced during the entire war."

C H A P T E R XVI

Aftermath of the Battle
(Those Who Escaped and Lived to Fight Again)

Elliott Goldstein

Though we did not know it at the time, those of us who returned to battle were the fortunate ones. The stress of combat is intense, but intermittent in nature. As those who became prisoners of war learned, the stress of captivity is pervasive and continuous. Only those of strong character and a will to live survived the inhumanities of being held in captivity by the Germans during the last months of the war.

These are the stories of the men who were returned to battle, the fortunate ones.

Randolph C. Pierson

After my escape from Parker's Crossroads, I trekked alone, through the dense Ardennes Forest, for two nights before blundering into an outpost of the 2nd SS Panzer Division in the darkness. My capture, by superior forces, was routine, if you can ever call getting captured routine.

At daybreak on the third morning, I was ushered into a warm tent and interrogated for quite some time by an SS major, an intelligence officer. The interrogation was both stern and intimidating. I was not comfortable during the interrogation and remained cautious with my answers, although I did give the enemy more than just my name, rank, and serial number. I conveyed a high degree of respect for this major at all times. To my surprise, my respect paid off when the interrogation was complete. While responding to my concerns, he assured me I would not be killed, I would be fed, my wounds would be treated, and I would be marched to the rear to become a prisoner of war.

Little did the SS major know I was already planning my escape even before I left his tent. I still did not relish the thought of becoming a prisoner of war. My chance to escape came later that day when a group of Americans was being marched to the rear. An 82nd Airborne trooper overpowered a guard, we killed him with his own bayonet, and fled into the thick woods unobserved by the other guards. Two days later, and miles away, I was exhausted, cold, hungry, and my wounded legs and frozen feet were hurting horribly. In desperation, I burrowed deeply to a snow covered haystack. Troubled sleep came quickly.

Was I awake, or was I dreaming? Loud and excited voices, coupled with the sight of an M-1 rifle pointed at my head made me realize I was awake. My captors were extremely nervous members of an infantry patrol from the 82nd Airborne Division whose mission was to capture German prisoners. The fact that this was an intelligence, and not a combat, patrol undoubtedly saved my life.

Reports from SHAEF Headquarters had alerted troops in the Manhay, Belgium, area to be on the lookout for English-speaking German soldiers, dressed in American uniforms, and carrying American arms. This report referred to "Operation Greif" and indicated the German soldiers involved in "Operation Greif" identified themselves to each other by wearing an American helmet liner, without the steel helmet. Earlier, to lighten my load, I had discarded my steel helmet and other heavy equipment as I struggled in the deep snow.

Since I had no steel helmet, the squad leader, and his men, were convinced I was a German soldier, involved in "Operation Greif," even though I answered all their check questions with a southern drawl, laced with spicy GI language. I was marched triumphantly to their company command post. There the company commander had his hands full and wanted no part of me, so I was marched back to battalion and received the same reception there. At regiment, I was placed under guard and taken to the regimental intelligence officer.

My interrogation by this Airborne officer was quick, brutal, and to the point. I was deemed to be a German spy, dressed in an American uniform. My sentence, "Take him out and shoot him!"

There was no way I was going to be led out into the snow and executed without a fight I launched into a heated tirade about the Civil War, Yankees and Southerners, the Mason-Dixon Line, called the Airborne officer a Damned Yankee who wanted me dead because I was a Rebel, and anything else I could think of at the moment. My ruckus produced results. First, the intelligence officer became livid with rage and started arguing with me.

185

Second, the noise caused by our heated debate caused a full colonel to enter the tent. His rank and presence had a calming effect on the situation. After he spoke with me briefly, I learned he was the regimental commander. He determined I was cold, hungry, and wounded, and made the decision to turn me over to his medical officer. The colonel spoke, so all could hear, and said he tended to believe my story, and thought I was actually a GI and not a German. However, he felt this decision should be made at a higher headquarters. Before he placed me under guard and released me to the medics, the colonel said something I will never forget. "Sergeant, you may be a good soldier, but you are a lousy judge of people. The officer you accused of being a Damned Yankee is from Alabama. I'm the Damned Yankee in the crowd, I am from upper New York State. Is there anything else you would like to say?" I was so relieved and dumbfounded, all I could say was, "No Sir."

My association with the medics of the 82nd Airborne Division and the staff of the medical facility for German prisoners of war where I remained for several days was very pleasant, but the "Intelligence Types" continued to give me a hard time. They simply refused to accept the fact that I was an American even though my name, rank, and serial number could be verified with the 106th Infantry Division records. Unfortunately, there were no records to be found.

This dilemma was finally solved the first week in January, and I was released from "American captivity" and rejoined what was left of the 589th at Chateau Xhos, Belgium. It was great to be an American again!

186

At the Chateau our future was not clear. Some people felt we would be reformed, and some felt we would be disbanded. I knew my feet still hurt and I also knew I had no control over what would happen. I decided to make myself scarce and let our new commanding officer, Major Goldstein, do whatever the army paid majors to do. He certainly did not need my help.

Most of my time while at the Chateau was spent at the overseers' cottage. The overseers, Louis and Madame Collinge, had four children. A 19 year-old son, Louis Jr., who was in England going to school, was hopefully removed from the war and not available to serve in the Belgian army. Their beautiful dark-haired, 17 year-old daughter Alice lived at home but attended a boarding school some twenty kilometers away. She thought nothing of riding her bicycle the forty kilometer roundtrip each week. Then there were the 13 year-old twins, Marie and Victor. With the twins, it was a case of mutual love at first sight. I always brought them chewing gum or sweets every time I visited the Collinge family.

Canned goods were plentiful for the troops at the Chateau, and fresh food was produced in quantity on the huge estate surrounding the enormous Chateau. This provided me with an opportunity to exchange canned goods, which Madame Collinge could store indefinitely, for fresh eggs, milk and cheese which were in short supply in our mess hall. This arrangement worked to the advantage of all parties involved.

Papa Louis was an infantryman in the Belgian army in World War I and had nothing good to say about the "Boche." We spent several evenings in front of his huge fireplace, drinking delicious wine and sipping Fina Cognac while Madame Collinge hovered in the background.

I am indebted to this loving Belgian family, who took me in and shared their life with me when I needed comforting the most. Unfortunately, the hostilities raged on and I was transferred to the 592nd Field Artillery Battalion and assigned to the XVIII Airborne Corps Artillery as a forward observer.

I was quickly assimilated into various regiments of the 82nd Airborne Division, usually serving with the regiment leading the attack. My initial feeling of being an outsider in an airborne unit quickly disappeared after I was able to assist the troopers with effective artillery support in some tight situations. Strange as it might seem, my being a noncommissioned officer, an enlisted man, also helped in my acceptance as a forward observer. I became friendly with the airborne noncommissioned officers and then easily earned the respect of the company grade officers with whom I worked. My moniker quickly became "Big Stick." Something to do with the quote from Teddy Roosevelt's foreign policy, "Walk gently, but carry a big stick." The troopers loved it when I used my "Big Stick," the United States Army Field Artillery, to help solve their problems.

Another thing I quickly realized, the offensive war to de-bulge the Bulge was entirely different from our prolonged holding action at Parker's Crossroads. In the attack mode, we hit and advanced, hit and advanced. We did not stay in one position long enough to really remember it, like I remember the action at Baraque de Fraiture.

In January, during the battle to regain St. Vith, I had an opportunity to demonstrate my "Big Stick" capability. My forward observation team and I were sitting on an observation post with not much to do when an Airborne infantry platoon leader, breathing heavily, pushed his way through the knee-deep snow to ask if I was a liaison officer. I told him no, I was a forward observer, and asked him to describe his problem. His lead squad, the one on attack, was pinned down in a ravine by a huge German tank, and he needed someone to neutralize the tank. We looked at his map, and he identified the problem area to me. Unfortunately, that particular target area could not be seen from our present location. This fact presented a problem.

The platoon leader looked desperate, so I called fire direction center for permission to close this observation post briefly while I relocated to another hill. My radio operator and I followed the lieutenant to an adjacent ridge. The view of the target area was perfect. Halfway across the ravine I could see the infantrymen lying flat in the snow; they were not dug in and were completely exposed. Across the ravine I could see what I thought was the largest battle tank in the world, a German King Tiger.

The Americans were hopelessly trapped in the open. They could neither advance nor retreat without taking heavy casualties. To make certain I knew what we were up against, I discussed the armor plate of the King Tiger with the platoon leader. He had done his homework and explained the armor well. To be effective, I decided to attack the Tiger with an eight-inch howitzer. The Tiger was stationary, and we could tell the motor was not running. In this frigid weather I assumed the Tiger would be difficult to start. I also knew I did not have much time to adjust fire upon this Tiger after the first round burst near the tank. Once moving, the Tiger would be almost impossible to hit with indirect fire.

My radioman transmitted to fire direction center my request for adjustment by an eight-inch howitzer. Concerned over the safety of the squad below, I left the radioman to complete the details of the mission and advised the platoon leader to contact his squad leader and tell his men to stay put because we would be firing directly over their heads. The platoon leader assured me his men would remain in place until he gave them permission to move.

What happened next was a textbook adjustment, straight from the field artillery school at Fort Sill, Oklahoma--a three-round adjustment and four rounds of "Fire For Effect." The howitzer crew, whoever they were, fired quickly and accurately. The four rounds slammed into the King Tiger just as it was beginning to move, producing brilliant flashes, dense black smoke, flying chunks of metal, and finally igniting the tank's remaining fuel. From our vantage point on the ridge, I witnessed an artilleryman's delight but a Panzer commander's hell. For the King Tiger and its crew, the war was over.

To my complete surprise, I was pulled out of combat and sent back to the 592nd the later part of January. There I was told, with no explanation, to find a Class A uniform, get cleaned up, procure a jeep, and get myself back to Stavelot, Belgium. On January 24, 1945, I was awarded a battlefield commission and promoted to second lieutenant along with two good friends from the 589th, Barney M. Alford, Jr. and Delbert T. Miller. After a hard night in Stavelot, "watering down" our brand new gold bars, the three of us returned to the front lines.

In my first combat assignment as a second lieuy, I received the most valued promotion gift a non airborne-qualified officer could receive. I was presented a new pair of jump boots by the regimental commander.

During the month of February all I did was move and shoot. All I remember until early March is a series of objectives to be taken--here a bridge, there a hill, here a hamlet, there a valley, next a crossroad, just one large blur. The monotony changed in early March when I was again relieved of my combat duties and sent back to Belgium--this time for glider training, and again, with no explanation.

My first impression of the air field where I was to train was, "Holy Cow, what is going on?" Half the transport planes in the Allied arsenal seemed to be gathered here. Along with the Curtis C46 and Douglas C47 transport aircraft were hordes of Waco CG-4A gliders parked all over the countryside. To me a person would have to be "Waco" to go up in one of those gliders. They looked like flying plywood coffins with flimsy fabric wings attached and equipped with a feeble landing gear straight from a junkyard. My driver put the icing on the cake when he asked innocently, "Lieutenant, you aren't going up in one of those things are you?"

After checking in and receiving temporary housing, my group was briefed on glider operations. The briefing officer stressed the fact that parachute infantry would be on the ground and have the landing area secure before the gliders brought in their cargoes. He informed us this was a training and assembly area for airborne operations, and we were to take part in training designed for vertical insertion of vehicles and artillery into a battle area.

It didn't take long to assimilate glider training. The basic training consisted of three instructions: enter the glider, sit in the designated seat, and fasten your seat harness. Shortly after my first take off, I added a fourth instruction: "Pray reverently!"

Even though I was barely twenty-one years old, I felt like an old man compared to the glider pilots. Their average age must have been nineteen or younger. I'll swear some of them were not even shaving yet. One pilot I flew with, or should I say glided with, wore pink and green uniforms, polished low-cut shoes, a 50-mission crushed air corps cap, and a 45-caliber semiautomatic pistol in a shoulder holster. He looked like the male lead in a Hollywood World War II propaganda movie. His main concern was how he was going to get back to his air base after he released his glider in a combat area.

On the ride back to Germany, I still wondered who had sent me to receive this glider indoctrination, and why. Many years later I realized how close I had come to being a forward observer in the Allied "Operation Varsity," which was later referred to as "The Airborne Bridge Across the Rhine." During this operation, the American airborne troops suffered severe losses.

Early April was most pleasant for me. I spent Easter week on leave in Paris. This was the first Easter celebration in Paris since 1939, and the people of Paris filled the churches, streets, bistros, and restaurants. This was a marvelous way for me temporarily to forget the war.

I left the battle for central Germany in mid April and detoured by the Chateau Xhos to visit with the Collinge family on the trip to Rennes, France to join the reactivated 589th Field Artillery Battalion. It didn't seem possible, but the twins had grown in the short time I had been gone. I left the Chateau teary-eyed and the twins were crying openly. We all realized we would never see each other again.

The war in Europe ended for me in Northern France, east of the Lorient submarine pens, where my battery was engaged in a holding action against German naval forces still stationed there. We celebrated VE Day late because the senior German officer in Lorient wished to negotiate separate surrender terms for his garrison. Although this delay was disappointing, we had a lively celebration when our VE Day finally arrived.

John R. Schaffner

The day after my escape from Parker's Crossroads, I located the small group of guys from the 589th who were not sent to Baraque de Fraiture. A miracle happened. In one of the vehicles, filled with duffel bags, I was lucky enough to find mine. Another miracle, clean underwear and socks.

I was transferred to the 592nd Field Artillery Battalion when Major Goldstein was ordered to disband the 589th. To my surprise, my assignment changed drastically. I was assigned to the 592nd fire direction center as a fire controller in this "medium artillery"155-mm. howitzer battalion. This duty was a "piece of cake", when compared to what I had previously experienced. Occasionally, I had to operate with a forward observation team. Fortunately for me, I did not have to pull this duty often because it was very risky business.

The 592nd was attached to the XVIII Airborne Corps Artillery and supported the counter attack on the northern flank of the "bulge" near Stavelot and Hunningen during the Allied drive which broke through the Siegfried Line for the second time. I stayed with this unit during the remainder of the time the XVIII Airborne Corps continued its attack toward central Germany. During this period, we did not stay in one position very long. The forward movement of the American army carried us farther east and deeper into Germany every dip.

Like everyone else, my feet were suffering from being cold and wet too often. I did not know it at the time, but I was suffering from the effects of frostbite, a carryover from those days in the wet foxholes around Baraque de Fraiture. Although I changed to dry socks whenever possible, it was not enough. I developed large, water-filled blisters on my feet which made it almost impossible to get my feet into combat boots. Although once I got my boots on, I seemed to do OK.

When I was off duty and had a chance to sleep, I removed my boots and stored them in the bedroll with me. The heat from my body kept the boots warm and soft and had a tendency to dry them also. I tried to air my feet as often as I could, but when they became warm, they started to itch. I used a good bit of GI foot powder, which seemed to help.

In late January or early February the time finally came for me to get a bath and change into clean underwear and socks. I was picked, along with about a truckload of GIs from the unit, to make a trip to Spa, Belgium for the cleanup. I can only presume we were selected because we were the dirtiest ones in the outfit at the time.

We must have been fairly near to Spa because the trip did not take very long. Spa had been a popular health resort prior to the war and was equipped with lavish Roman-style baths, fed by the local mineral springs. Our truck stopped in front of a building, which reminded me of a Roman temple, marble columns in front, et al. When my turn came to take a bath, a woman dressed in a white outfit, much like a hospital worker, led me down a marble corridor to a vacant bathroom. This room contained a huge bathtub centered on an elevated base. The female attendant immediately started both water taps and promptly left the room.

The bathtub was about one-half full when I stripped down to my birthday suit and prepared to take my bath. Suddenly the attendant reentered the room, stuck her hand into the water, turned and surveyed me, shook her head, and said, "NO! NO! Water too hot!" I didn't know what to do, so I just stood there and watched while she ran more cold water. When the water temperature was proper; she turned, smiled sweetly, motioned toward the tub, and said, "OK".

The bathing experience was great, but in retrospect, the experience would have been even better if she had stayed and washed my back and if I had been able to change into a nice clean uniform rather than putting on my old cruddy one again.

On a few other occasions we had the chance to bathe in "Engineer's Showers". This was a setup where an Engineer unit built a maze of water pipes, equipped with showerheads spaced a few feet apart, near a river. Water was pumped from the river, through a filtering system, and then heated for use in the showers. The installation was normally screened by a surrounding tarp. This type shower arrangement could handle a large group of guys in a short period of time. Army efficiency at its best!

Near the end of February, our unit moved into the remains of a village to take up a support position for the advancing infantry. As usual, the first order of business was to find the most comfortable "accommodations" available. While inspecting one of the remaining houses still intact, I heard one of the guys call to come upstairs and take a look at what he had just discovered. When I arrived, he was busy checking for boobytraps. He had discovered a storage space in the wall, hidden behind a bed. Using our flashlights we could see about two or three dozen bottles and several pieces of cured meat. Now, really afraid of boobytraps, we inspected the dark area thoroughly. Finding none, we cautiously tied a long string around a bottleneck, and from a safe distance, gently pulled the string. The bottle fell over as we pulled it into the room, but nothing happened. We tried again, with the same results.

Once emptied of its contents, the hiding place in the wall provided us with fine brandies, cognac, and hams, similar to the kind we refer to as "Smithfield" in the states. That night we feasted on ham fried in brandy. This meal was not bad and provided us with a welcome break from our normal meal of "C" rations.

The remaining booze was "divvied up" among the guys in the squad, each one storing his bottles in his bedroll. Some of the booze actually survived until V-E Day, but all surviving bottles died an honorable soldier's death during our enthusiastic V-E Day celebration.

About the first of April I found out the 589th was to be reorganized in France. The plan was to return all surviving members to the unit and bring the battalion back to authorized strength with replacements. This news was welcome and made me feel good when I learned I would be assigned to "A" Battery with First Lieutenant Ted Klendl as my battery commander. I felt like I was going "home".

During the reorganization period near Rennes, France, the officers tried to keep the men busy. "Idle hands are hands of the Devil", is probably more true in the army than in civilian life. We "veterans" had been in and out of combat for almost five months now, and much to the distaste of the battery officers, amused ourselves and bedeviled the replacements by igniting magnesium flares and detonating hand grenades which had been deactivated by removing the explosive powder.

Early in May, I accompanied the battery to the "Lorient Pocket" to reinforce the 870th Field Artillery Battalion. At both Lorient and St. Nazaire, the enemy held the cities and about 100 square miles of adjacent French countryside. The Germans had established elaborate minefields and defensive installations guarding the approaches to their submarine pens.

The surrender negotiations with the German garrison commander in Lorient was not completed for several days after the official V-Day in Europe. When the German garrison finally capitulated officially, "A" Battery had one hell of a party. Everyone but the battery commander and some key noncommissioned officers got roaring drunk. Why not? We had earned it. For Germany and for us, the War was over!

Barney M. Alford. Jr.

In the process of escaping from Parker's Crossroads, suddenly I found myself alone. Luckily for me, I finally stumbled upon a squad of parachute infantry from the 82nd Airborne Division. They took me back to their company command post and gave me some hot food. After I ate they let me go to sleep, and I got my first good rest in several days.

Feeling better, and incidentally feeling safer, I told them I was a howitzer section chief. The next thing I knew, I was literally shanghaied into their supporting artillery battalion. I don't really remember the battalion designation, but I think it was the 463rd Parachute Field Artillery Battalion. There are several things I do especially remember about the battery that I served with for several weeks. First, they were very happy to get a trained section chief--they had lots of new guys in their outfit. Second, they were armed with 75-mm. pack artillery pieces which could be disassembled into several packages and dropped from transport planes and reassembled on the ground. These howitzers were good little weapons, but compared to the 105-mm. howitzers to which I was accustomed, they seemed like popguns. And third, once they got hold of me, they did everything they could to keep me.

My experience with the airborne troops made a favorable and lasting impression on me; however, I didn't know what happened to my friends at Parker's Crossroads and wanted to find out so I kept after the officers to get me returned to the 589th.

On January 24, I was ordered to Stavelot, Belgium, and unexpectedly received a battlefield promotion to second lieutenant. I was glad to see two of my friends, Delbert Miller and Randy Pierson, in Stavelot. They were from headquarters battery of the 589th and received battlefield promotions also. The three of us were reassigned to units in XVIII Airborne Corps.

199

The same order promoted all three of us. In the process of becoming an officer, the army issues the candidate a different serial number which begins with a zero. The three new numbers assigned to us were sequential. Since my name begins with an A, they assigned me the lower number, Miller the next, and Pierson the highest. Army lore is full of stories of rank among second lieutenants, so I will add one more. Miller never gave me a hard time, but Randy did on occasion. When I got into an argument with Randy, I always pointed out, "Pierson, I know our date of rank is the same, but I outrank you by two serial numbers." That settled the argument most of the time!

My promotional leave to Paris, France was a great experience. I cannot explain how quickly a soldier can became a civilian again in Paris. The sights of Paris in the spring quickly erase the horrors of war. I enjoyed the sightseeing, the nightlife, the good wine and fine cognac, but the thing I remember best is the stage show I saw at the famous Follies Bergere.

During the battle to de-bulge the "Bulge" and the subsequent Rhineland and Central Germany campaigns, I served as both a firing battery officer and a forward observer for various units in XVIII Airborne Corps Artillery. I can remember destroying bunkers, firing on troops in the open, shooting into enemy strong points in villages, and neutralizing crossroads, but don't ask me for details. This part of the war is one big blur to me.

At the reorganization of the 589th Field Artillery Battalion at Rennes, France, I was assigned to "B" Battery, and was almost immediately sent to the

Lorient Pocket near the German submarine pens on the coast of France. Our mission was to help keep the German naval garrison, still occupying this area, from escaping. While we were there, the German high command signed the unconditional surrender demanded by the Allies, and the rest of the world celebrated V-E Day. Not us however--we had to wait for the local German commander to negotiate his own surrender. This took several days.

When this finally happened, we had our own V-E Day celebration. Man, what a party!

Elliott Goldstein

By going north on Highway N30, the road to Manhay, I managed to work my way to the remnants of the 589th Field Artillery Battalion. We rendezvoused at Eronheid where some of those who had escaped joined us. We proceeded north to Spreemont and were billeted in houses in the village. We were welcomed warmly and enjoyed the opportunity of sleeping in a real bed with a down comforter--quite an improvement over our previous sleeping conditions. The next day we moved to Dolembruex where we were again billeted in private homes. I couldn't understand why I was given the master bedroom while the owners slept in the basement. I found out after dark when I was awakened by the sound of V-1 buzz bombs overhead. They were aimed at the railroad yards in Liege but occasionally fell short, and the house was on the flight path of the V-I's. I learned that as long as you could hear the putt-putt of the bomb, which sounded like an outboard motor, you were safe. When the sound stopped, the bomb dropped. Fortunately, all passed the house putt-putting away.

We were told that we would be reorganized, and we were permitted to draw new equipment. The belongings of many of us were restored to us, having been kept safely for us in the rear echelon. We were then ordered to Chateau Xhos, a large chateau south of Liege occupied by the D'Oultremont family. The chateau had so many rooms that the younger Countess D'Oultremont said she'd never been in half of them. There were several farm houses around the castle, and personnel were billeted in the farm houses and in the chateau itself. We were welcomed since we gave the occupants a feeling of safety. All of the men in the D'Oultremont family had left, and only the two D'Oultremont ladies, the older Countess and her daughter-in-law, remained, along with servants and farm personnel. Their only request was that we take off our shoes before we went into the parquet-floored ballroom. I was assigned an office off the library, and put together a roster of those present, reported in to division artillery, and wrote the after action report and recommendations for officer commissions and decorations. We were notified that instead of being reorganized, the battalion would be broken up and the personnel assigned to other organizations. The majority were assigned to the 591st and 592nd Field Artillery Battalions, which were almost intact.

On January 1, pursuant to orders, I joined the 592nd Field Artillery as Battalion Executive Officer and stayed with that battalion until mid April. I was now again able to fight as an artilleryman. It is certainly preferable to be firing indirect fire in support of an offensive than to be shooting directly at people you can see and who can see and fire at you. The 592nd was assigned to XVIII Airborne Corps Artillery as were a number of other battalions. The corps artillery's mission was to support various units of the XVIII Airborne Corps in their advance.

We moved into Germany, going into position, firing and then moving again as the infantry moved. When we came to the area in which the 422nd Infantry had surrendered, I was able to reconnoiter the terrain southeast of Schönberg to the Skyland Drive. There, in a bowl-like depression, I saw the corpses of a number of American GIs, undoubtedly former members of the 106th Division. Many of them had been mutilated, their throats cut, their genitals cut off and shoved in their mouths. It was a ghastly sight. I've never seen this incident reported, for reasons that I don't know, but it was like the Malmedy massacre. We wanted our infantry to take German prisoners for interrogation in order to find out what was in front of us. I found that our soldiers were so inflamed by German atrocities that they were shooting Germans who surrendered. But our troops finally accepted the order that they should not harm prisoners, but send them to the rear for interrogation.

As we advanced into Germany, we became a well-oiled machine. We were able to do what we'd been trained to do, and since we were a 155-howitzer battalion, we were far enough from the enemy to be out of rifle range. My relationship with Colonel

Weber, who was the Commanding Officer of the 592nd, was very good, so much so that he tried to persuade me to remain in the Army after the war ended. When I asked why in the world I would want to do that, he explained to me how great life in the peacetime Army was. He played on the Army polo team and spent a large part of the fall in California, the winter in Florida, the spring in France and the summer in Newport, R.I. playing polo. At his home station, Fort Meyer, his day consisted of taking the first sergeants report at reveille, riding around the area where the men were training, returning for lunch at 11:00 and playing polo in the afternoon. The Army furnished him with a string of polo ponies. He said, "Only a millionaire could live the way I do." I told him there was only one catch--I couldn't play polo, so I respectfully declined his invitation.

Since we were the most forward of the corps artillery and were in contact with forward observers, we had the opportunity of massing artillery on an objective. If we were given an assignment to bombard a particular target at 6:00 am., we would notify all the other battalions, they would compute the time necessary for their rounds to reach the target as we did, and then would fire without command so that all of the rounds would arrive on the target at almost exactly the same time. The sound of all those shells passing over was awesome.

In one incident I had prepared a time on target barrage for 6:00 a.m. on a defended position on a steep embankment overlooking a river to prepare for an attack by paratroopers who were to climb a cliff and attack. At 5:30 we got a message from the airborne troops that they had occupied the position. They had decided that the best way to attack the position was to climb the embankment at night and surprise the Germans rather than wait for a barrage before attacking. When they arrived at their objective, they found the Germans had pulled out. Fortunately, we were able to stop the barrage.

As we got farther into Germany, we went into a static position. I don't know why, probably for all units to link up for a final advance. The Germans were putting up a good fight, and we were receiving artillery rounds every day. Fortunately, there were few casualties. (Slit trenches provided adequate cover from everything except a direct hit.) Each morning General McMahon, the Division Artillery Commander, would call me and ask how things were going. I would say, "Just fine, General, we've got a few rounds coming in, but no one has been hit." His reply was always, "Well, keep up the good work, I'll be up to see you tomorrow." This was repeated every day for nearly a week without a visit until finally I said, "General, we haven't received a single incoming round."

Needless to say, General McMahon's smiling face was soon in the area, and we were all glad to see him.

As things quieted down, leaves were granted. I got a leave to Paris, where I found that those of us who had been in combat were a curiosity. I was wearing the jacket which I had gotten from an armored force officer. When I was knocked down by a mortar shell explosion, shell fragments went through the jacket and left holes that were clearly made by shell fragments. An enlisted man working in a rear-echelon office saw me on the street and asked if he could buy my jacket. I asked him why he wanted a beat-up jacket like mine. He replied that it had been in combat, and it would be helpful to him. When I told him it was not for sale, he made me an offer I couldn't refuse, which paid for my leave in Paris. I hope the jacket was successful for whatever he had in mind. The war was far away from Paris, and it had much of its old charm. I think everyone who got leave to Paris fell in love with it.

In the middle of April, we were ordered back to the Quiberon Peninsula on the Atlantic coast of France in the vicinity of Rennes for the reorganization of the 106th Division. I was reassigned to the 589th Field Artillery, but was detailed to reorganize the 422nd Infantry, probably the best assignment I had in the Army. I was given a cadre of about thirty officers and three hundred noncommissioned officers and enlisted men, the survivors of the 422nd Infantry Regiment. We soon set up tents to house the headquarters and troops. We received about three hundred men and ten or twelve officers every day and soon had three full battalions. I found out how luxurious it is to be an infantry regimental commander in a noncombat environment. Each time my sergeant major found that we were receiving a chef, we looked over his qualifications. If he came from a good restaurant, we assigned him to the headquarters mess. Conversely, each time an officer came in who ranked me I sent him to a battalion. There we sat in the richest farm country of France with chefs from some of the best restaurants in the United States. As Winston Churchill said about having six corporate directorships, this job was like relaxing in a warm bath. But it was soon to end. A regular Army lieutenant colonel arrived, and I realized that the party was over. I turned over command to him and returned to the 589th. Major Parker had returned from the hospital and now commanded the battalion, and I again became executive officer.

Our first assignment was to support a Free French battalion which was supposedly containing a German garrison which had been holed up in Lorient providing protection for German submarine pens. The first night we went into position some of the cannoneers decided to walk up to where the infantry was located and find out what was going on. They kept walking until they came to a small cottage whose occupants ran out and greeted them warmly. They were invited in and given cake and wine. While they were trying to communicate, they saw a group of men in gray uniforms marching by. Their host said "Les Boche". The Americans were horrified, but they were assured there was nothing to worry about. They finally returned to the battalion, unharmed. We found out that the Free French unit stayed in position during the day and at night retreated to the nearest town where they spent the evening in restaurants and bars.

There the war ended. The Germans surrendered, and we fell heir to their well-stocked wine and alcohol cellars. Every man received two or more bottles of his choice. Included in the loot were some bottles of fifty-year old Napoleon brandy. Since most people had no use for that, I swapped my Scotch and bourbon for

Napoleon brandy, the best trophy of the war that I received.

Thereafter, the battalion moved up to a position overlooking the Rhine for training. We went into a fixed position, got into comfortable quarters, and prepared for our next assignment in the Pacific. Those who had sufficient points (based on service overseas, battle stars, decorations, and number of children) were put into a separate group to go home. The points needed increased with rank and were 85 for a major. Since we had no children, my points did not add up to 85, the magic number. At that time I received a message that Colonel Charles Reid, a former Chief Justice of the Supreme Court of Georgia, and prior to that time a partner in Powell, Goldstein, Frazer & Murphy, the firm that I had practiced with, wanted me to come to Frankfort to become a part of his staff. He was assigned as Chief of Property Control in the U.S. delegation to the Allied Control Council. I went to Frankfort and was assigned as his deputy chief and after the office was organized, moved to Berlin.

The Allied Control Council, consisting of the four powers, the United States, England, France, and Russia, was supposed to govern Germany and Berlin as a unit. However, each country had an area to administer, and the City of Berlin never came under united control. The American delegation to the Allied Control Council was extremely top heavy. Every general and colonel without an assignment gravitated to the Council, and there were no second lieutenants. Colonel Reid was seldom in the office, and I ran the Property Control Division. One of my assignments was to meet with my opposite numbers from the other three powers to prepare laws for Germany. One Of the laws that I drafted provided for compensation to be paid to those whose property had been seized by the Nazis. After going through the routine for several months, I found that the law would not be put into effect because the Russians were administering their territory as a separate sector rather than as a part of the joint government.

The last assignment I received was to write a letter to General Hildring, who was in charge of the military government for Germany, for the signature of General Clay, the United States member of the Allied Control Council. I was told that General Hildring had asked for a report on military government by the Allied Control Council. 'I prepared a three-paragraph letter which General Clay signed. By that time I had sufficient points to be eligible for discharge. When I reached the number of points that would permit me to leave, I made up my mind that I did not want to go back to the States in command of troops on a troop ship. I persuaded my superior to issue orders for me to proceed to the Pentagon for thirty days to recruit personnel for Berlin. I had an uneventful but nauseating trip back on a Liberty ship which had been hauling grain, the dregs of which were rotting in the hold. But it was better than having to ride herd on soldiers who were getting out of the army. I arrived in Washington and reported to the Pentagon. After I reported in, I only received one assignment--to reply to a very nice letter General Clay had written to General Hildring, the reply to be prepared for General

Hildring's signature. I told them I'd have no difficulty writing such a letter since I'd written the original letter to which it was a response. Apparently General Hildring was satisfied with my work, because he signed it.

The rest of my tour at the Pentagon was spent enjoying my reunion with my wife Harriet, visiting with old friends who were stationed in Washington, and getting back into civilian life. I was discharged from the Army in February of 1946, exactly five years from the date of my induction into federal service. I had received a promotion to Lieutenant Colonel, so I returned home with silver oak leaves. I was asked to join the reserves, but I told them the last time I responded to such a request and joined the National Guard to get my service over with, I had gone halfway around the world and didn't get out for five years. My conclusion was that I wasn't joining anything ever again--not even the American Legion or the Veterans of Foreign Wars.

CHAPTER XVII

Aftermath of the Battle-Brutality

(Soldiers Who Were Captured and Became Prisoners of War in Stalags or Work Camps)

Elliott Goldstein

The stories of these individual members of the 589th who became prisoners of war, and survived, are quite varied. Most of these recollections are the bitter sweet tales of enlisted men who were subjected to indescribable hardships. These men all possessed the one basic quality necessary in time of war, the will to survive! These are their stories.

Calvin V. Abbott

After we were captured, they marched us for miles and miles with no food. We were then put on a train in a boxcar with no room to sit down. There was one little window at each end of the boxcar, about six by twelve inches in size, covered with barbed wire. We had one bucket in the middle of the boxcar for body waste. They carried us to Gerolstein and placed us in a work camp. At Gerolstein there was a railroad yard, down in the valley, where we were made to work day and night on the tracks.

After months there, the Germans heard the Americans were coming close, so they marched us day and night to a prison camp in Limburg. We stayed there for awhile--I don't remember how long. One day the commander of the prison gathered us on a platform and told us that Hitler had ordered all prisoners to be shot, but he said he was not going to shoot us. They then herded us out of camp, marched us for a day or two, then stopped in a farm village where they put us in a big barn. There were guards and barbed wire all around the barn. On March 29, 1945, American tanks came roaring in. We were freed, sent to a field hospital, and taken care of.

I weighed 165 pounds before I was captured, 97 pounds when liberated.

John C. Rain

I spent Christmas in a town in Luxembourg, with Captain Brown. They moved me to Prum, Germany next, then from there to Gerolstein. I reached Limburg after the bombing and was a prisoner in Stalags 12A, 10B, and 10C. I was liberated from Stalag 10C on May 5, 1945, by units of the British army, then flown to Brussels, cleaned up, and issued a complete English winter uniform. I was moved from Brussels by train to Camp Lucky Strike and spent two weeks on a ship to New York.

In the states I received a sixty-day recuperation leave and then reported to Fort Sam Houston in San Antonio, Texas. There I was assigned to the Army Test Center for Foreign Equipment in Fort Bragg, N.C. where I handled material classified SECRET.

On November 21, 1945, I was discharged from the army at Fort Bragg, as a staff sergeant.

John F. Gatens

On April 28, 1945 I was liberated from a Stalag near Bremen, Germany by Welsh guards. What a wonderful group of guys. They couldn't do enough for us. The next day we were taken to Brussels, Belgium. After our clothes were burned, we got a complete delousing; then a hot shower. I would have paid a million dollars for it. After a short physical and a complete set of English uniforms, we finally started through the chow line. (Something I had been looking forward to for a long time). It wasn't a case of getting as much as you wanted. The portions were very small. They had guards at each end of the line, to make sure that you didn't go through more than once. We were pretty mad about that until they explained to us that the first group of released prisoners of war were given all they wanted, and many became very sick and a few of them died because their bodies could not handle a load of rich food. We were fed six meals a day but very little at a time.

After a few days, we were flown to Camp Lucky Strike, LeHavre, France. Finally back into American hands. This was better than any comical movie ever made. Here was this group of American GIs in English uniforms and not far away was a group of English soldiers in American uniforms. Naturally if you saw someone you knew, you mixed in with the crowd to say hello. The officers had their hands full trying to get all the Americans in one group and the English in another.

While I was at Lucky Strike, the Germans surrendered (VE Day). The Camp went crazy. Their war was finally over!

We were put on a convoy of Liberty Ships for the trip home. What a catastrophe this was. These ships were originally scheduled to take German prisoners to the states, then quickly converted to take us. So you know there were no comforts involved. The convoy was traveling under blackout conditions, even though the war was over. There were still German submarines around, and they may not have received word that hostilities had ceased.

It was very foggy most of the time. A slight turn in course was signaled by blinker light because radio silence was being observed. Some of the ships got the signal and some did not. Our ship was sideswiped on one occasion and rammed in the stern on another. I thought I was going to die in the middle of the Atlantic Ocean. After twenty-one days, we finally made it to New York.

On November 15, 1945, I was discharged from the army.

Charles P. Jacelon

When we were forced from the command post at Parker's Crossroads a German tank commander waved us through, between tanks, and as prisoners of war we were collected behind the German spearhead and directed to march on the roadway toward Houffalize.

214

We marched a mile or two and were herded into the basement of a farm house. I had a few ration crackers in my pocket, and I shared them with Jeff Pafford. On the 24th, we were marched to Houffalize and spent the night in a schoolhouse. The next day we walked to Prum. While we were in Prum, we were given picks and shovels and were told to fill in bomb craters and pot holes.

A German officer in a small command car said his car was inadequate for the battlefield job it was supposed to do and was only good for driving the streets of Paris or New York. I told him it was too late for that. He had never seen those cities. He laughed, gave me a cigarette, wished me good luck, and drove off.

The air raid sirens went off and the work detail guards all ran for the cellars. I found many jars of preserved vegetables and filled the inner lining of my GI overcoat with jars, carried the coat over my arm, and returned to the building we were quartered in during the night. After body heat had thawed the contents of the jars, I shared my loot with the men near me. The next day we marched to Gerolstein, which was a staging area and railhead where preceding prisoners of war from the earlier days of the Bulge had entrained. I was to spend the first six weeks of my captivity here.

The building that the German army was using as a transient prisoner-of-war enclosure was a factory/warehouse complex. There were built-in bins lining the walls on two floors and a room near the center stairs on the first floor that senior noncommissioned officers had taken over. Both floors were crowded with prisoners of war with narrow paths through the groups. I have no idea how many people were in the building, but the coverage was like a popular beach on a busy day. The toilet was a brick enclosure in the yard, with no cover. Some nights the guards would not let us go to this enclosure and a large garbage can was placed near the door. It overflowed and ran into the sleeping areas.

One of the men I knew and remember was the Battalion Sergeant Major, Master Sergeant Hill, who was sick when we got there (I would imagine with influenza). He received no care, and died after some few days. Jeff Pafford was a friend with whom I shared a foxhole at Parker's Crossroads. He had a light-weight body, and he was evacuated with a trainload of sick prisoners. He died later in a Limburg prisoner-of-war camp, I'm sure there were others who suffered the same fate, but these two were closest to me.

Our daily fare was one-eighth of a loaf of brown bread and a container, helmet, canteen cup, or whatever was available, of very thin soup. The bread, cut into eight pieces, would be given to a group, and each man would be given a number. One designated individual would then hold a portion of bread under a cloth cover, and another designee would call a number. The person holding the called number would get the piece of bread being held under the cloth cover. We repeated this process until each man had received his portion of the loaf of bread.

I soon learned there was nothing edible to be found in the prisoner-of-war enclosure and took every opportunity to get out and into the city. One German family had a small grocery store on the main street, with living quarters upstairs over the store. The building had been bombed on Christmas day, and the lady had been trapped in the wreckage for hours. Their supply of food was stored in the cellar, and they wanted help to locate and remove the food from the wreckage. Four prisoners of war, including me, were designated to help them, and at noon each day the lady would give us a bowl of GOOD soup. This luxury lasted about a week.

My friend Jeff Pafford went out with a contingent of sick people. They were loaded on a train for Limburg. A week or two later the remaining prisoners of war in Gerolstein were evacuated just ahead of the advancing American army. We marched ten to fifteen miles a day through Mayen and Coblenz to Limburg. In the camp there, I filled out a prisoner-of-war registration card. This was a structured camp. Food was provided by a central kitchen, which kept all the Red Cross bundles and prepared the contents. One day, in addition to the bowl of soup, or whatever, each man got half a box of raisins or prunes. I took the raisins, then went around picking up all the prune pits I could find. I broke open the pits and ate the little seed nuts inside.

At Limburg I developed an infection on the fourth finger, left hand, and had to have my wedding ring filed off by a British prisoner-of-war doctor. During the Limburg days, I went out on a burial detail and saw the dog tags of one of the deceased. The dog tags belonged to Hugh Mayes. Hugh had been my radioman in our forward observation party.

When the American army was closing in on Limburg, we were evacuated by train, but we did not get very far. We were bombed. We took turnips from storage pits on farms and ate them raw. We rolled under the freight cars when planes appeared. We spelled out "POW" by standing in lines and bending over. The trains stopped in tunnels overnight. After a day or two the train was abandoned and we started walking. I helped a new prisoner-of-war, who was wounded, and could not keep up. The guard tried to hurry us along, but I kept hanging back:. He finally left us and I turned up a side street. We found a church and slept awhile. When I left the church, a German civilian told me American tanks were on Main Street. When I arrived at Main Street, I waved to the tankers of the 2nd Armored Division.

A chaplain in a jeep evacuated me to a French labor compound, where I took a bath, got some food, and slept the night. The next morning I turned myself in to the medics, who commandeered two or three houses side by side. The medics told the occupants to collect their valuables and get out. The occupants were given one-half hour. The citizens tried to get out with their bedding, but were told to leave it. The medics established a field hospital there, and I was the first patient.

I stayed at this location overnight, where I got cleaned up, deloused, bathed, and pajamaed. The next day I was moved by ambulance to the first airfield liberated east of the Rhine and flown by a medical evacuation plane to Paris. After an overnight stay in Paris, I was flown to southern England for a four-week stay for stabilization. When able to fly, I was then flown to Walter Reed Hospital.

Stalag 12A in Limburg was the first prisoner-of-war camp liberated. *Life Magazine* had pictures of American soldiers looking like skeletons. As a prisoner of war I lost sixty pounds. Malnutrition and the accompanying dysentery produced some life-long problems for me. My teeth were never healthy after this experience, and my fingers do not have full sensitivity.

However, I have been very fortunate that I did not develop serious life-long deficiencies. After stabilization and many tests at Walter Reed Hospital, I was placed on a long convalescent leave. Upon my return to Washington, I was transferred to the rehabilitation hospital on Long Island.

On January 11, 1946, I was discharged from the army and awarded fifty-percent Veterans Administration disability compensation. Time in service, five years, two months, and twenty-six days.

Eldon L. Miedema

After being taken prisoner at Parker's Crossroads, I, with about twelve to fourteen other American prisoners, was marched all night and then questioned by German officers. The next day, we were marched to Houffalize, where we were held two days. The Germans had not given us anything to eat or drink, except water out of roadside ditches. The civilians of Houffalize were permitted to give us some stewed potatoes and black bread on Christmas day. Then we were marched to Prum, still without anything else to eat, in bitter cold weather. Here we were locked up on the third floor of a schoolhouse, without any stove or heat of any kind. There was immense suffering; men with frozen feet and trench foot. Here we were fed--ten men to a small paper sack of crackers, almost like oyster crackers. It came down to about ten of these crackers per man per day. Water came from streams or ditches.

While in Prum, I worked with other prisoners on the railroads in the daytime. We were strafed and bombed by fighter planes at different times, and several in our group were killed and wounded. The wounded were left to lie on the cold, unheated third floor of our prison with starvation rations and little or no medical care.

After about a week in Prum, we were marched to Gerolstein, which was even worse. There were several hundred GIs here, locked up in a two-story warehouse. We were fed water mixed with flour from a bombed-out storeroom. The only eating utensil we had was one tin can for each man, which we never had a chance to wash. It wasn't long before most of the men had dysentery. I was awful sick with dysentery, frozen feet, and from drinking water out of ditches, but the Germans still worked everyone who could so much as stand. We worked on the railroad and various other jobs.

Several boys died here from malnutrition and various other ailments brought on by starvation. I had lost approximately fifty pounds in weight by this time, had feet which were terribly frozen, and with severe dysentery, I was really sick. The Germans finally decided they had better send the sick and disabled out of there as they could not work and by this time quite a few of us had died.

Eventually, after being locked up in 40 and 8 boxcars, fifty men to the car, which was an awful mess, with all the boys sick with dysentery, and no food or water for four days, we arrived at Stalag 12A in Limburg, Germany the last of January 1945. After we arrived in Limburg, we were registered with the International Red Cross.

We were fed once a day, eight men to a loaf of black bread and some slop they called soup. We slept on the floor of an old barracks, in filthy straw, that was alive with lice, bedbugs, etc. While here, I had pleurisy, acute hepatitis, frozen feet, and lost still more weight from dysentery and a general rundown condition.

The latter part of March, 1945, the American army was advancing on Limburg, so the Germans evacuated the Stalag. I escaped the first night while on the march and hid out in the woods near Weilburg, Germany. The next day, the 2nd Infantry Division took Weilburg, and I made my way into Weilburg and an aid station.

Here I started my way back to England to hospital plant 4128. I weighed 112 pounds when arriving there. I had weighed more than 180 pounds when I left the states. I had a fever of 102 to 104 degrees for three months before finally starting on the road to recovery. Finally, I was in the hospital in England for about two months, and then flown to the states.

After arriving in America, I spent four months in Schick General before being moved to Percy Jones Convalescent Hospital. I was discharged from the army January 23, 1946.

Bernard C. Stohmier

I was taken prisoner at Baraque de Fraiture, Belgium on December 24, 1944, at about 1600 hours. On Christmas Day, I was given a black cigar by my captors. I was marched to Prum, Germany and then to Gerolstein, where I was interrogated by the Germans in a stone castle. During the interrogation, I was offered the opportunity to join the German army by an officer who had been educated in Chicago.

When I told him I had sworn allegiance to the Allies, he said he understood, and told me he could arrange for me to be sent to the Russian front. I, of course, refused, and he had me remove my overshoes and strip to the waist. He then ordered me to stand for some time on a balcony outside the building, exposed to the bitter cold, with my hands in the air. I cannot understand why I did not freeze to death during this experience.

Later they sent me to a labor camp near Trier, Germany, in the Moselle River Valley. I was assigned to hard labor and cut logs that were to be made into charcoal blocks. In the spring of 1945 the American army was pushing rapidly toward Trier, and I was moved to Stalag 12A near Limburg, Germany. Later the American advance caused the Germans to vacate Stalag 12A, and I was put in a boxcar with about eighty other prisoners, with standing room only.

On the way to Frankfort, Germany, the engine of our train was disabled by an Allied air attack. As time went on, there was more and more room in the boxcar because many of the prisoners died of malnutrition, dehydration, dysentery, and exposure to the cold. After nine days without food or water, I was liberated by elements of the 9th Armored Division.

I was then flown to Paris, France. The next day I was flown to the 119th General Hospital in England. There I received many transfusions of blood, plasma, and intravenous liquids because of severe dehydration. In June, 1945 I was flown to the states, and received treatment, convalescence and rehabilitation in several army hospitals before I was discharged from the service in 1946.

CHAPTER XVIII

Aftermath of the Battle-Cruelty

(Officers Who Were Captured and Became Prisoners of War in Oflags)

Thomas P. Kelly, Jr

While the Oflags (officer camps) were undoubtedly more tolerable than the Stalags (soldier camps), they were completely lacking in comforts and amenities. Officers were not required (or permitted) to work, but that had its disadvantages--enlisted men who worked outside of the camps were often able to scrounge food while at work; officers had no such opportunities (unless they had a friend in the kitchen, as we shall see). These are the stories of two 589th officers who were POWs.

Arthur Brown

Shortly after capture, I was escorted away from Baraque de Fraiture and marched down the road towards Samree, Belgium. The guard was armed only with a pistol, which he kept in his holster. Although the thought of escape occurred to me, I was not in any shape to try anything rash. I was cold, wet, hungry, limping (from the clubbing I received at the hands of my captor) and very tired. Further, the enemy was everywhere and the winter weather was not conducive to lying concealed outdoors. Again, if I could have gotten the upper hand, it would have been necessary to kill my captor to make an effective getaway, and the thought of this one-on-one also deterred me.

After walking a mile or two, we came to a field command post. They had me empty my pockets in which my captain's bars had been placed. They allowed me to keep both my insignia of rank and my I.D. card. My apprehension of what they might do to me began to fade, as the treatment afforded me as an officer captive was always good from that time on.

After proceeding farther on the road to the German rear, we finally came to a chateau that had been commandeered, probably as a division forward headquarters. We were most likely at the medieval chateau at La Roche, although the Germans were not exactly orienting me regarding the route of march. To the contrary, they blindfolded me for a time. My captors took me up to their officers' quarters where dinner was in progress, and allowed me to help myself. Nobody seemed to notice me and no one appeared to be standing guard. This treatment was a subtle method of softening me up and also an illustration of the respect with which the Germans accorded an officer. I wonder what treatment the allied army was giving the German officers under similar circumstances. My guess is that the German prisoners were not being mistreated, but neither were they being given this old world treatment.

After a leisurely meal (and the fare was good), an SS officer approached me and asked me to follow him. He not only spoke English, but with an unmistakable

Brooklyn accent. He later admitted to having been brought up on Long Island. The questioning by this intelligence officer was non-military, mostly political. He seemed to be particularly interested in President Roosevelt. The fellow had a sense of humor, as at one point he told me that I was not supposed to tell him something. It was difficult to stick to name, rank, and serial number replies as the interrogator was very disarming. The thrust of my replies to these questions was that our side had a strong will to defeat the Germans. At any rate, I was very ill informed as to what was going on around me and would not have been able to tell him anything valuable if he had tortured me. When the interview was ended, I was returned to the basement of the chateau where there was a large group of American prisoners spending the night.

The next day we marched some distance and our captors put us inside of a building. My hands were very cold, and a guard helped open a tin of food they had furnished us. I remember cursing the can opener that came with the can as I could not figure out how such a small piece of metal could do the job. It was Christmas Eve and one of the guards, with a soulful look on his face, put up a tree in the house. It did not have any ornaments of course, but we all had a better feeling about the Germans at this point. Our guards were a bunch of guys just like us doing their job, and obviously would rather have been at home with their loved ones.

The next day was Christmas, and after the day's march we were herded into a schoolhouse for the night. The building where we were staying was close to the Luxembourg border as the textbooks were written in French. I was able to read a bit of that language, and learned for the first time that the climate of the region was moderated by the Gulf Stream. It is hard for me to realize that the latitude in the Ardennes is about equal to the lower end of Hudson Bay, Canada, and if it were not for the Gulf Stream, the life style of the inhabitants might be somewhat different.

Marching on the next day we arrived at Gerolstein. At this place the Germans were collecting prisoners and forming marching transport headed inland to the prisoner-of-war camps. There were many wounded Americans in Gerolstein who were not receiving treatment, some in very bad shape. As I was utterly helpless to do anything about the situation, this was one of the most depressing scenes of the war to me.

My recollections of the trip to the prison camp at Limburg are hazy. We must have traveled about 125 miles, mostly on foot. The walking was much preferable to riding in a truck, however. The one night that we were transported by truck I froze my feet. The prisoners were riding in the back of the truck which had a steel bed, and we did not have room to move around and stimulate circulation. At our destination, I spent the rest of the night with my shoes off trying to rub some circulation back into my feet. To this day, I can't sit around, even in the summer time, without something on my feet to keep them from feeling numb.

I never once felt heat from that December to May. One night I remember we prisoners were in an unheated building and a small aircraft flew over and bombed the windows out of the house. I can remember being very angry about the cold wind the explosion let in, and seemingly not at all upset about the attempted murder. We slept on the floor like curled-up Alaskan huskies, no man daring to move lest he should lose the body warmth of the two next to him. Our hips were so sore and legs so stiff that we could hardly stand by the next morning.

I remember walking along a hilly country road and approaching a small village below us. Fire lanes were neatly cut at intervals through the majestic forests. The ancient trees spired toward the sky, each trying to outdo the next one. I later was to discover that the Germans worship trees like people in India revere their cows. A German would rather freeze than chop down a tree for firewood.

As the sun was finally shining, the Allies had started up their bombers again. This activity had been suspended for several weeks during the very bad weather in the early days of the Bulge attack launched by the enemy. We stood by the roadside and watched stick after stick of large bombs from high flying Allied aircraft being dropped on the village. I do not know why this target was selected, because we later went through the village and I do not remember seeing anything of a miliary or industrial nature that would have attracted an attack. It could have been a railroad or motor transport center or something with no visible presence.

In the village the ambulances were just gathering up some wounded residents from the ground, and we helped load these civilians into trucks. Otherwise the streets were deserted as the rest of the populace had sought refuge from the bombing in the hills nearby. The houses in the village were very close to the street. I was so hungry that I darted out of line, risking the wrath of our guards, to steal a handful of those excellent German Christmas cookies by reaching through the open window of one of the houses on the street.

But for the kindness of the German villagers in the countryside through which we passed on the way to the Rhine River, we prisoners may not have survived the long march to Stalag 12A. One night in a small village near Mayen, we were fed a very nutritious and delicious meal. I have since learned that the people in this area were in dire straits themselves at the time. The villagers placed a huge iron kettle on the fire and prepared the best stew I can ever remember eating (no disrespect, Mom). Not having had any hot food for two weeks or so, indeed very little food at all, we all ate until we could eat no more. A remarkable thing happened to me while waiting for this repast. I walked into the village pub next door to where we were billeted, sat down and asked for a glass of wine. My request was honored and the villagers treated me as though I were a regular customer except, of course, I had no money with which to pay.

It was near the end of December when we arrived at the confluence of the Rhine and Moselle Rivers at Coblenz. This German city, with an estimated prewar population of 300,000, had been devastated by the Allied bombing. I did not see a building standing. Dead bodies lay in the streets. Only a few survivors peered out of cellar windows. We hurried through the city on foot fearing the next wave of bombers, which mercifully did not arrive while we were there.

The bridge over the Rhine at Coblenz was still standing. We proceeded across on our way to Limburg's Stalag 12A where we had reservations for the winter. The last twenty miles to Limburg were getting rough on some of the air corps pilots in our group of prisoners, as they had not experienced much conditioning for this type of activity. One pilot developed cramps, and the guards were going to leave him by the roadside in the snow. I got him up piggyback and carried him the last several miles to camp. (Later this man was to ignore me in prison camp, due to what quirk of human nature I am not able to fathom.)

I had foolishly abandoned my overcoat which had been given to me by my German captors near the front. One day the sun shone brightly and the extra weight, while hiking, seemed to be an unnecessary burden not demanded at this instant by the temperature. Fortunately, the prison camp issued me another from their plentiful stock of American GI (Government Issue) clothing.

After the initial assault I received upon my capture, at no time while I was a prisoner of war was I physically mistreated. We all, prisoners and guards alike, suffered from insufficient food. The captive officers were in a different compound from the captive enlisted men. The compound next to ours contained Russian soldiers. The Russians always seemed to have plenty of potatoes which they would trade for

231

cigarettes. Among ourselves, at one time I saw a gold Parker pen traded for a few cigarettes.

Life in the prison camp was boring for the most part. The officers were not sent out on work details into town and thus did not have the opportunity to steal food as did some of the enlisted men. The food situation gradually deteriorated over the next four months. One meal a day was always the rule, and this did not come until about 1700. At first the soup was made of potatoes and greens and laced with meat (I hesitate to venture a guess as to what kind of meat). In addition, each man had a half loaf of bread at first. Gradually the meat disappeared from the soup and finally we were down to one-tenth of a loaf of bread per day. Incidentally, the bread was not exactly fresh baked, as one loaf that I was eating in 1945 was date stamped 1939. The bread was extremely dry, about the consistency of sawdust, but therefore did not mold. From our barracks window we could see a dirt mound of potatoes, extremely large, which the prison authorities nevertheless invaded sparingly. The thinking on their part was probably that with the deteriorating situation on the side of the Germans, there would not be much chance to replace the food supply once it was exhausted.

The sanitation was probably the worst physical aspect of prison camp. The stench of the outbuilding designed for the purpose of receiving body wastes was so overwhelming it took a strong stomach to even go in. There was fortunately an option, which while being more primitive in concept, was less nauseating.

Everyone had body lice. There was a washroom with running water, which like everything else was unheated. However, I never actually saw anyone taking a bath under these conditions. Shaving was accomplished by holding a razor blade in your hand without a holder, soap, or mirror.

Frequently at night the air raid sirens would sound. They started down the valley (of the Lahn River) from the direction of the Rhine in the vicinity of Coblenz. I can hear them now, getting nearer and nearer, as one little village after another took up the cry. Then pretty soon we would hear the drone of the bombers and the clatter of anti-aircraft guns as the planes came toward us. Limburg was a prime target, and the bullseye was the railroad yard just west of the prison camp.

One night a stray bomb or two came into the prison camp grounds. We all hit the deck and got under the cots. Some were wounded and killed in the barracks next to us. We did not know if the "friendly" bombers were aware of our proximity to the rail yards, but I'm sure this would not have stopped them. If you don't want to get shot by your own countrymen, do not get captured: "C'est La Guerre".

It is true that I can sleep under almost any conditions. To keep the pangs of hunger from being so painful, I took to napping late in the afternoon while we were waiting for the guards to bring the day's chow. When I heard a stir in the crowd, it would be time to wake up and get my share.

As the winter wore on and the sun shone bright enough to take off some of our clothing outdoors, we engaged in the sport of squashing lice. These

233

unwelcome guests did not really depart until we were repatriated and went through the delousing baths and had a fresh change of clothes.

When the Allied armies had first crossed the bridge at Remagen, the authorities at Stalag 12A prepared to move us deeper into Germany. It was bitter cold, and they gave us some straw to load in the open slatted cattle cars of the railroad. This enhancement was supposed to keep us from freezing. As we were putting the straw into the car, an air raid started. Most of the men and the guards took to the surrounding hillsides. For some reason I decided I would take my chances with the bombs rather than freeze and continued to load the hay into the car to which I was assigned. At the last moment, I had a change of heart and took off running towards the nearest hill. The blast of a 500-pound bomb impeded my progress blowing me into the air about ten feet. I jumped up and continued to run until I caught up with another prisoner. He looked at me and his eyes opened wide in horror. Only then did I realize there was a hole in my jacket and blood was oozing out of my chest. A bomb fragment had struck me in the right lung.

The guards took me back to the prison camp. A German doctor looked at me and shook his head. He gave me the only treatment that I assume was available, consisting of a band-aid over the opening and one shot each of penicillin and morphine. They told me these medicines were the last in camp. That night the pain was excruciating. However, I was still better off than the man in the bed next to me. He did not survive the night.

My lung was collapsed and an American doctor prisoner advised me to lie as still as possible for a week or so until the lung reinflated. I am certain that the only thing that saved me from infection was the continuous cold, in which I am convinced that no germ could survive. The fragment was to stay in my chest until 1958. At that late date a bout of pneumonia required removal of this foreign object in my bronchial tube to stop the hemorrhaging and allow drainage. The army has me classified as twenty percent disabled, but except for occasional discomfort, I have always been able to do pretty much as I wanted physically. At any rate this incident may have shortened the war for me as the Germans were not able to move me farther into the fatherland.

Finally the prison camp in Limburg became no longer tenable. The Allied armies were across the Rhine River in force at Remagen, and moving swiftly towards Limburg and points east. The order came down for everybody capable of moving, or being moved, to evacuate. There were some that were too weak or sick to leave. A transport of about one thousand prisoners of all ranks was assembled. We were loaded on trains, again with the officers in a separate boxcar. It was getting on toward the end of April and mercifully the weather was moderating.

After a day or so of backing and filling, mostly at night to avoid the bombers, the boxcars were left standing in daylight on an elevated ridge. This made us a perfect target for strafing, as the planes could come in low. It was not long before some American P38s and P51s took advantage of this "sitting duck" situation. The air corps obviously did not know the train contained only American prisoners (with a few English). We were locked in the cars, and on the first pass by the aircraft, our guards took off to the ditches alongside the tracks.

A medical corps captain and I watched with fascination the incoming planes through cracks in the boxcar, while our comrades hit the floor. I did not see how the floor on an elevated car would serve as much protection against strafing or bombing. As it turned out, the car next to us was strafed with multiple 50 calibers which the American mustangs carried in their wings. The car looked like a sieve on later examination. The carnage in this car was terrible, At this point a brave guard came back and opened the door to the officers' car, and we spread down the tracks opening car doors and releasing our enlisted men.

As the planes came over again, I dove in to the furrow of a nearby ploughed field with bullets splatting in the freshly-tilled soil all around me. At this point I suggested we form the letters "P O W" with the prisoners. This came fairly naturally to me, being a former Drum Major of the Duke University band. The tactics of spelling out our identity with human backs was successful as the planes wiggled their wings in recognition and left us to deal with our wounded. We had absolutely no medical facilities, but the German doctor did what he could under the circumstances.

After the strafing experience, the guards decided to park the train in a tunnel. We were in there for over three days without water; however, that was better than the alternative of being in the open and bombed.

Finally movement by train was abandoned. As the senior American officer, I was instructed by the German officer in charge of the prisoners, to form my men up into one hundred men units with an American officer in charge of each contingent and move out.

I called all of the officers forward (mostly second lieutenants), and told them to each take one hundred men and line up. When the group was ready, we paused and sang "Onward Christian Soldiers." On the road one man was too weak to go on. I ordered four men to carry him on a blanket stretcher and exhorted them not to abandon him or he would perish. We took off and marched some time before coming to a halt for a rest. I overheard a German guard saying the Allied army was bypassing us to the north. The guards acted like they had been drinking. Apparently they knew the end, for them, was not far off. After we had started to move again, I got to thinking about the opportunity to escape now. Before thinking any further, I boldly stepped out to the side of the column to call the American officers forward to the head of the line to meet me. As I guessed, the guards watched without interfering. None of them spoke enough English to understand what I was saying. I informed the officers of the situation and told them to pass the word to the men to slip quietly into the surrounding woods as the opportunity presented itself.

That evening we marched into a small village. An English chaplain, who had been a prisoner for four years, and I went into the adjoining house and the villager fixed us a huge platter of bacon and eggs. This was the first hen fruit to reach my stomach in nearly

237

six months. My digestive tract was so shrunken and out of order that the solid rich food made me violently ill.

Several of us hid in a barn loft, and as the prisoner transport was slowly breaking up, apparently we were not missed. I went down into the nearby public building, which to my surprise was occupied by regular German soldiers. When I burst in on them I was so startled that, without thinking, I offered one of them an American cigarette. This action disarmed him so that he allowed me to beat a hasty retreat. The next day I set out walking by myself, and remember seeing one of our former guards with a very depressed look on his face, bicycling his way home.

Soon the point vehicle of an American outfit came along. It was a jeep loaded with three men, armed to the teeth with automatic weapons. They were scouting way out in front of their main force. They picked me up and we went into the village. There were some German soldiers milling about in what had now become a no-mans-land, but they did not make any aggressive move towards us, even though they were also armed. We parked our vehicle and entered a tavern where some villagers were having their morning drinks. We lined the locals up against a wall at gunpoint and proceeded to order cine beir (a beer).

My liberators took me to a field hospital where other American prisoners were being processed. They had delousing baths and new clothes on a mass production basis. From there I was flown to a permanent hospital at Reims to recuperate. My diagnosis was malnutrition, with a weight loss down to approximately 115 pounds from my pre-prisoner weight of about 165. One of the few things I remember about the hospital was the amazement and behind-the-back whispers of the others as they watched me heap food onto my plate.

It would be some time before my digestive system would come back to some semblance of normalcy. After several weeks, orders came down for me to proceed to the port of embarkation via Paris. The mode of transportation to that city was an all-night train. In my car there was one "closet" for "Femmes & Hommes". I kept this tied up for most of the night while food passed rapidly through what had once been my digestive tract. The locals were not too pleased with my performance as they were frequently lined up outside the door when I emerged.

In Paris I discovered my orders were inadvertently undated. This meant I could have stayed in Paris indefinitely as a guest of the United States government, lost to the World, so to speak. But after a quick go at the cathedral of Notre Dame and a night at the Follies Bergere (the latter tame by modern standards), I longed to get back to my bride and the ultra civilization of the USA.

So I proceeded on to Camp Lucky Strike, the staging area for ships headed west. We were quartered in a tent city. There I purchased a new dress uniform, complete with the insignia to which I was now entitled, having been in three battles and wounded. At this time I did not know the government had also awarded me the Silver Star. But at any rate all this began to make me feel more like an officer and a soldier of some experience.

After a short wait, my turn came up to board ship for home. Again, there was a strange twist to my departure and journey. Another thousand-man transport was formed, of which I was again the senior American officer (still only 28 years old). Aboard ship, of course, the navy was in charge. There were approximately thirty officers junior, and reporting, to me among the service men being shipped home (mostly ex-prisoners). I set up a roster for officer-of-the-watch to cover the whole trip to New York, being careful to leave myself off the list. Therefore, except for one incident, I had nothing to do except enjoy the voyage all the way home.

We sailed across the English Channel to Southampton and put in for supplies and more men. As we were tied up there, the war in Europe came to an end (VE, or Victory in Europe Day). We were not allowed to go ashore and celebrate, but the attitude of the soldiers was one of war weariness and this did not seem to be a great hardship.

After several days at sea, the rolling crap game in the hold got out of hand and fights broke out. I donned a sidearm and descended into the hold where the bunks were stacked five high. The smell of seasickness was pervasive. The trouble was quickly allayed by a combination of rank, bluff, volume and profanity.

Thomas P. Kelly, Jr.

After spending the night in a schoolhouse in Gerolstein, early on the morning of December 21, we were marched to a railroad sidetrack where a line of empty freight cars awaited us. We were separated into groups of approximately 100 and each group was ordered to enter a car. For the uninitiated, European boxcars bear little resemblance to their American counterparts. As the tracks are narrower, so are the cars; and they are only a little more than half the length of freight cars in the United States.

Militarily they are designated 40 and 8 cars, designed to transport 40 men or 8 horses. With approximately 100 men in each car, only one-third of us could sit on the floor at one time and the rest remained standing. The only way we could sleep was to lie on each other, which also was the only way we could stay warm enough to sleep. The boxcar was to be our home for at least the next ten days (if I kept an account of the days, I no longer remember the number).

Our train left Gerolstein that morning traveling east but with frequent prolonged stops. As would be expected, the use of main line tracks by our train was apparently assigned the lowest possible priority. The door on the right side of our car was never locked, probably for the convenience of our guards who placed a large can of water on board each morning unless the train was moving, and a crate of food (potatoes or other vegetables and black bread) through the door on most evenings. There was a hole in the floor at one end

241

of the car that served as the rest room. Everyone remained on board at all times; we had been told that anyone who exited the door would be shot by the guards.

On either December 22nd or 23rd, we passed through Coblenz with much switching from track to track, and then we were on the way east again. I remember Christmas Day well because it was the first time I had seen the sun since I had arrived in Germany. We were again on a side track in a small village (probably in the vicinity of Arnstein) and we were out of water. As the senior officer in our car (we had been able to sort each other out by that time) I was nominated to attempt to replenish our supply. I slid the door open and called to a soldier who was lounging on a bench outside of the minuscule railway station, "Vasser, vasser" several times, rattling our empty water can. The soldier did not bother to get up, but glanced in my direction and called back something that sounded like "Alles Kuputt."

We were to hear this expression many times in the coming months. Literally translated it meant, "Everything is broken", but the way it was said I am sure it meant, "You Americans have been bombing us so heavily that nothing works, so you will have to take the consequences." So be it. We derived a great deal of satisfaction from the fact that our Air Force was destroying the enemy's facilities even if it meant that we were deprived of the necessities of life. A few days later we were not so sure.

We had been in the massive railroad yards at Limberg for several nights and were beginning to think

242

that we were going no farther, although we had received no information regarding our destination. Shortly after dark, we heard the distant roar of many airplane engines, and as the sound became almost deafening due to its proximity we realized that the railroad yard we occupied was the probable target. Within seconds bombs were dropping all around us, but primarily in the expanse of the yard on the right side of our car. When the car began to rock like a boat in heavy seas due to nearby explosions, several of the younger soldiers rose and ran across prone bodies toward the door. Before I realized that I was doing so, I yelled a command for them to stop and get down. I was surprised that I had asserted authority that I did not have, but even more surprised that the young soldiers obeyed my command. If they had left the car or even had opened the door they would have been exposing themselves and the rest of us to injury or death.

After about five minutes the bombing stopped and the noise of the engines receded. No one in our car was hurt, but we learned later that a door on one of the cars in our train was blown in and there were casualties in the car. We also were told that, fortunately, there was a military hospital near the railroad yard where they were taken for treatment. I wondered if their injuries would prove to be a blessing in disguise. I still do not know.

We left Limberg one afternoon while I was in a group conversing with a French officer, who had been captured in our sector of the front while serving as liaison from a Free French unit attached to our Corps.

He said he could not stand any more humiliation at the hands of the Germans and intended to leave the train that night. He explained that he had escaped from a prison train years before by jumping from the doorway while the train had slowed to a speed of less than 20 kilometers per hour during the night time when the guards on the last car could not see him jump and start firing. He said that he wanted someone to go with him because two persons were safer than one; there was always a chance that one could be hurt after hitting the ground and the second person could assist the injured one in making his escape.

I remembered that when I had been captured in maneuvers I had escaped by jumping from my captor's command car when it slowed to make a turn. That frivolous escapade could not be compared to jumping from a moving train in the middle of an enemy country abounding with armed guards and a hostile civilian population and into an icy snow-covered ditch in temperature around 20 degrees below zero. Nevertheless, I weighed the odds and decided that the deeper I traveled into Germany the less chance I would have to get back to freedom. And here was a chance to have as a companion an experienced escape artist who spoke German like a native. I told him I would go with him.

We discussed techniques of falling after jumping from a moving vehicle (we agreed that the approved method is to wait for an open area, land on the feet but immediately fall on one shoulder and roll with your head off the ground but without attempting to stop until you have lost momentum). We then bided our

244

time. When it was fully dark the French officer (whose name I cannot remember, but we will call him Renee') moved to the door on the right side of the car and motioned to me to follow him. I did so and together we opened the door about two feet. The cold wind invaded the car as Renee' crouched poised on the threshold, and I stood immediately behind him. We were moving at about 20 miles an hour and I assumed Renee' was waiting for a decrease in speed, but after about five minutes he pulled the door closed.

"Have you changed your mind about escaping?", I asked.

"Yes, at this time", he said.

I asked why and he said that the bitter cold and the prospect of many days and nights without food or warmth dissuaded him.

"There will be a better occasion", he said. I did not say any more, but I was secretly glad that he hadn't jumped. I had said a prayer and I undoubtedly would have followed him if he had leaped into the darkness. As uncomfortable and unhappy as I was, the freight car was far more friendly than a snow bank in a completely hostile and vengeful world. And a snow bank is the best that we could have hoped for.

We arrived finally at the town of Bad Orb where the train stopped on a side track and we were ordered from the cars. Two prisoners had died in my car during the day before our arrival; one of them was my former Headquarters Battery Sergeant Major, a regular army career soldier who had been promoted to Warrant Officer just before we left England. I wondered what was in store for those of us who were still alive, and if Warrant Officer Smith was lucky that he would never find out.

From the town we were marched up a hilly and icy road about two miles to a stalag (prison camp for enlisted men) where there were prisoners of many nationalities. We were directed into a large common room where potatoes, turnips and carrots were dumped on the floor and a few loaves of black bread were placed on a table. We were told that we could eat, and although we had not enjoyed an opportunity to do so in at least two days, I was again struck by the lack of discipline of the young soldiers who fell on the food like sharks in a feeding frenzy until the last shred and crumb had been devoured.

The enlisted men were segregated from the officers and marched to another area of the stalag. (The only occasions when we saw them thereafter were at the morning assemblies when all prisoners were gathered in an open area and the guards responsible for each group reported on all present and otherwise accounted for.) The officers were then ordered into their separate quarters and the field officers (majors and lieutenant colonels) were provided a single room with a pot-bellied, coal-burning stove in the center and double bunks against all of the walls. We were to occupy this new home, a vast improvement over our former, mobile one, for about a week.

Early on the next morning, we were taken to a large hall where we were searched. This was no mean undertaking, even for the rough and clumsy soldiers assigned the task. I was wearing three suits of long underwear, the outer two made of wool, the same number and composition of socks on each foot and three pairs of gloves, the inner pair being fur lined and the outer pair being wool mittens. I had on a wool uniform and a battle jacket made of a canvas-like material, over which I wore a down jacket my wife had bought for me at Abercrombe & Fitch and a knee length trench coat with a coarse wool lining. Despite all of this protection, I was freezing all of the time, night and day.

Probing through the padding the soldier searching me was able to feel and extract all of my personal belongings except one item: the hand compass I had thrust into the thick down of my Abercrombe & Fitch jacket before again sealing the opening. It was to serve me and others in good stead.

But predictably, the searchers were not the brightest of the Germans we had encountered, or would thereafter. After the soldier had removed all of my other personal belongings, including a wrist watch, a note pad and attached pencil, a handkerchief and a dozen other articles, and had placed them on a table, he went a few steps away to get a container in which to place them. The moment he turned his back I retrieved all of the items specifically identified above and stuffed them in my pockets and then resumed the position of attention in which he had left me. He returned and dumped the remaining items in the container without noticing that the more useful ones were missing. I finally brought all of them home when I returned to America.

We soon learned that the coal that was placed outside our room each morning, consisting of 5 or 6 lumps the size of a large fist, were all we would get that day. The first day we burned them in the morning and had no means of heating the day's single meal, a thin potato soup served at about 1700 hours. Our requests for more coal were not dignified by a response. The second day we were again running short and I decided to go out in search of the source of supply. I found the coal pile in the enlisted men's area about a quarter of a mile away and to my surprise there was no guard. I picked up the largest piece I could find, about the size of my head, and started back to our room. I had not gone twenty steps when I remembered why, despite the three pairs of gloves, we kept our hands in our pockets while outdoors. My hands began to freeze in their open positions on both sides of the lump of coal. Before I was half-way to the room they had passed through a period of excruciating pain, and were completely numb, frozen to and around the lump of coal. I couldn't even drop my burden and abandon the project and it took two hours, and all of the lump of coal, to become able to move my fingers again. I then understood why there was no guard on the coal pile.

I do not recall how many days we were in the stalag. But one morning it was unusually cold and at the daily assembly Klinck and I began sparring to keep the blood circulating and the joints movable. After a two minute round, won by my smaller but very nimble opponent, I noticed a very sharp pain in my left chest. I thought I had pulled a muscle but by the time we were dismissed the pain had intensified and I realized it was internal and not muscular. I went to the building designated as the stalag hospital and my temperature was 104 degrees. I was diagnosed as a case of pneumonia and assigned a bunk in the only building in the compound with a temperature above freezing.

The 422nd Infantry Regimental Surgeon was a very personable individual, and a competent and enterprising physician. When we had arrived at the stalag several days earlier he had demanded that everyone, including those of us who outranked him, turn in to the medical detachment all of their "wound tablets". In those days before penicillin and the many other present-day antibiotics it had long been known that sulfa drugs would combat infections and in the combat zones everyone was issued sulfa tablets to be taken in the event of a wound of any seriousness. I was to learn that they also cured bacterial pneumonia.

The pain in the left chest did not subside for 24 hours, but as a result of massive doses of wound tablets, the pain was almost gone by the following evening. The regimental surgeon came to my bedside that night and after taking vital signs (normal temperature, pulse and respiration) and close questioning, he said:

"You are not out of the woods yet. You are lucky not to have developed pneumonia in your right lung, but it could happen at any time. However, if your vital signs stay within normal limits, you are well enough to be discharged tomorrow morning if you elect to go with the other officers of your division to an oflag (prison camp for officers). I don't know where it is or how many days it will take you to get there or what will happen to your pneumonia on the way, but I will discharge you if you stay well overnight and decide to leave with your group."

It did not take me long to make a decision. Even though I realized that 44 hours was a phenomenally short time within which to recover from pneumonia, and before marching away in sub-zero temperature, the alternative was unacceptable. I was not going to abandon my friends. The only redeeming aspect of my situation was that we were all in it together.

I left the relative warmth of the hospital room at 0800 hours on the following morning and found all of the officers I had been captured with and a few newcomers, even two or three of my own, assembling for the march to the railroad station. I was free of pain but very weak; I was consoled by my recollection that it was only about two miles to the railroad and down hill all the way.

We were again packed into boxcars, but our number was considerably less than a thousand and there were not as many in each car. The trip to Hammelburg required only 24 hours and we were marched from there to Oflag XIII B, occupying a former cavalry training center with many permanent buildings and a huge arena in which troopers learned horsemanship. We were told that if we were caught trying to escape we would be shot there.

The days passed slowly in the oflag. We were each given a loaf of bread, a coarse, damp, black lump of baked dough and sawdust, each Monday, and it was supposed to last a week. Whether it did or not, no more was issued until the following Monday. We each ate two slices of our loaf for breakfast every morning

250

after toasting it on top of our pot-bellied stove. The only other food provided was a bucket of soup, either potato, cabbage, turnip or carrot, or mixtures thereof, every evening. There was enough for each of us to have one bowl and I never saw one turned down; even if it was tasteless it was still hot and presumably had some nutritional value. We had enough coal for two fires, one in the evening which died during the night and one when we awoke. Each of us was allotted two blankets, and since the temperature in the room before daylight was near or below freezing, we slept in our clothes. We shed them once a month, when we were privileged to take a shower in the latrine building, which was about 100 yards from our barracks.

The field officers (except the two full colonels) were allotted a room in the northeast corner of the same hall in which about one hundred company and battery grade officers slept. I knew most of the officers in the room, including Lieutenant Colonels Klinck, Lackey, Puett and perhaps one or two others, and Majors Scales (who had commanded a battalion of the 422nd), Tietze (my former survey officer and later S-3 of the 590th)and others. Puett had operated a restaurant for several years in his native Georgia and as a consequence of this experience, he was designated as the oflag mess officer and charged with supervision of the cooks who prepared the evening soup. He also signed for the provisions furnished to the kitchen. On one occasion, he gave his roommates a surprise dinner party; he brought in a pot of stew containing pork and whole new potatoes that was the first real meal I had eaten since December 18, 1944. And the last for a long time, because while the quantity of the ingredients Puett had received was extremely limited and the Germans probably expected him to do just what he did, we all felt a little guilty. I remember that Lackey and I both suggested that he not do it again, and he didn't. But he didn't seem to lose as much weight as the rest of us (in my case 35 pounds, and not more than 5 of it had been excess weight).

Shortly after our arrival at the oflag, another group of American officers was brought in from a prison camp in Poland that was in danger of being overrun by the Russians. Among them was a Colonel Paul Goode, who was senior to Colonel Cavender [7] and, therefore, became the ranking American officer in the oflag, and Lieutenant Colonel John Waters, who was the husband of General George S. Patton's elder daughter. Waters had been captured in the battle of Kasserine Pass in north Africa in 1942 and had been a prisoner of war for over two years.

The camp in Poland had been organized by Colonel Goode, who had designated Johnny Waters as his executive officer. Now as the senior officer in Oflag XIII B, he renewed the organization, retaining Waters as executive officer and appointing other officers to various staff positions. I was appointed Judge Advocate, probably because I was the ranking lawyer,

---

[7] None of us had seen or heard anything about Colonel Descheneaux since the night we had spent at Auw (December 19-20). The Germans had spirited him away during the night for their own purposes, but I learned later that he had survived his POW experience.

but no one ever advised me of my duties and I don't remember ever performing any. The Germans provided all the law that the oflag was allowed.

What helped to make life bearable for most of us was the proximity of the compound where 3800 Yugoslav officers were quartered southeast of our area. They had been captured in the spring of 1941, when the Germans overran a hostile Yugoslavia to protect their right flank and rear in their projected invasion of Russia. Ninety percent of these prisoners of War were Serbs from Serbia and Montenegro and they had almost as little regard for the other ten percent, consisting principally of Croats and Muslims, as they had for Germans. We made many friendships with these delightful Serbian officers who thought they owed us a debt of gratitude because they had survived for almost four years on American Red Cross food packages. Inasmuch as we never received any ("alles kaputt") they shared with us to the extent that they could do so and stay alive.

We had received orders not to fraternize with the Yugoslavs, but the latter early made holes in and under the interior fence where the German guards never ventured, and soon we were visiting back and forth every night. We were supposed to be in our own rooms by 2200 hours and remain there the rest of the night, and since one elevated guard post over the latrine had a direct view into our entrance, we usually complied. But some of the Serbs had musical instruments and frequently played them in their quarters, singing and dancing (with each other) until 2150 hours or later. They served us coffee and sometimes a cookie from their Red Cross packages, and the evening hours passed much more quickly and enjoyably than the dreary and tedious hours of daylight under the baleful eyes of the guards.

There was one young Serbian lieutenant with whom I formed a close and lasting friendship (he came to America after the War and established a business in Miami, Florida, visiting me in Tampa on one occasion). His name was Johan Johanovic (John Johnson) and he, like most of his compatriots, hated the Germans for what they had done to his country and despised the Croats, Muslims, Hertzegovinans and Slovenes for the same reasons his parents and grandparents did; reasons that were very difficult for him to articulate but to him very compelling. He especially condemned Tito, who was then leading Communist forces from Croatia against his hero, Mihailovic and the Chetnics. He expected and predicted the separation of the Yugoslav states and the wars that have raged between them since the death of Tito.

There was a fence of heavy wires about three meters (10 feet) high around the entire compound. Certain of the wires were electrified with sufficient voltage to cause serious injury or death upon contact. Before our arrival, one Serbian officer had been killed during an alleged escape attempt, although it apparently was not clear whether he was electrocuted or shot to death by rifle fire from the guard towers. In either event, it was agreed by those of us (and we were surprisingly few) who were escape-minded that attempting to break through the fence, in daylight or under the searchlights at night, was not the way to go. Although they were very secretive about their intentions, I learned of two groups who were planning to escape and eventually I asked for, and was granted, permission to join them both. The leader of one group was the same French officer, Renee', who had dared me to jump off the train with him, and then had failed to jump. But I got the impression that this time he would see it through. We all agreed, however, that it would take some diversion, a fire or an explosion in the compound, of sufficient seriousness to require the services of the tower guards, to render an escape through the fence feasible or even possible.

Several of us spent many hours with Renee' during the daytime learning conversational French. My one course in that language at the University of Florida was helpful, but hardly decisive. I was never able to master, or understand, any French beyond a few pleasantries, and my pronunciation evoked many patient corrections from my mentor. I reluctantly decided that the soft, musical language of the French was not for me. But I refused to try to learn the harsh, guttural language of the Germans, even though it might be helpful if I succeeded in escaping from the oflag (in the event this proved to be true).

We had been told that among the offenses for which we would be executed was possession of a radio; nevertheless I learned after a week or two in the oflag that one of the American officers had a small set and antenna that permitted him to hear broadcasts by BBC from London. I did not know the name of the officer and did not want to (torturing of prisoners to obtain useful information was a practice that was not unknown to our German captors). But I was eager to hear reports regarding the progress of the war and sought out reliable sources of such information. During late January, and in February, I was told that the Americans were holding in the west and attacking the German salient from the north and south, threatening to cut off the enemy armies in Belgium and forcing their withdrawal. The retreat of the Germans was slow in bitter fighting, but was steady. Finally, the bulge was only a curve in the line and the American armies were back on the Schnee Eifel. We then were told that there was a successful crossing of the Rhine. Our spirits were lifted immeasurably.

An even more reliable indication of favorable developments at the front was the changing attitude of some of our guards. When we first arrived they were uniformly hostile and aggressive and occasionally abusive; it was obvious that they still believed that Germany would win the war. But early in March there was a gradual change. The guard assigned to our building who formerly had stomped through the hall every morning, glaring from side to side, now entered smiling with many "guten morgens". He even stopped to chat occasionally, but not about the war.

Another indication of the changing attitude of the Germans was a summons I received to visit with a civilian official in the oflag. I was escorted to a small office near the home of the commanding general and met there a pleasant, middle-aged official (probably the Gauleiter of the district) who spoke excellent English. He invited me to sit across from him at his desk and offered me an American cigarette, which I accepted with alacrity. (Cigarettes were the only form of currency in the oflag; there was a package in each Red Cross box and the Serbs who didn't smoke frequently gave them to the Americans. The non-smokers traded them to the addicts for bread in a very lively, daily exchange. I was not involved in that market; I smoked those that came my way, but didn't trade away my food to get them.) When I had lighted up (the official struck and held the lighter for me), the German said,

"I hope you realize that our armies in the east are fighting your war for you."

I said, "No, I don't realize that. I thought it was your war."

He smiled tolerantly. "You must know", he said, "that the Russians are determined to extend Communism throughout the world. Do you want America to become a communist state?"

"Of course not", I said, "but that will never happen."

"If the Russians defeat Germany on the battlefield and take over our industrial facilities, you won't be able to stop them when they come after you. Neither will Great Britain", he said.

I had about finished my cigarette and was ready to terminate the conversation. "Look", I said, "we Americans can fight only one war at a time. Right now we are fighting you Germans because you declared war on us. We are going to win this one, and then if we have to fight another one, we will win that one too."

257

Again the tolerant smile. "Which nation do you believe America is more similar to, Germany or Russia?"

"There are more people from Germany in America than there are people from Russia, and I am glad of it", I said.

This time his smile was genuine. "Think about it", he said, "Of course, you think more like we do than like the Russians do, and you should be helping us to defeat them or some day we will have to help you to do so."

I could only say, "I'm sorry. You started it and the Russians are helping us to finish it. We can fight only one war at a time."

He stood and extended his hand. I shook it; after all, he had given me a cigarette, and lighted it.

All of the guards were not conciliatory or reconciled to defeat. One named Hans Germann (a name I did not learn until much later) was in the tower over the latrine on a night late in March. A few minutes after 2200 hours, an American infantry lieutenant, whose name I do not recall, was approaching our hall where his bunk was located and in doing so was visible to the guard for a distance of about 40 feet. Just in front of our entrance he was hit in the abdomen by a shot from the tower. We heard the shot and his cry for help and two of us went out and carried him to our room. We removed his torn and bloody clothing and saw a gaping hole in his abdomen that exposed his bowel. It was grey in color and there was very little internal bleeding. We knew he needed medical attention but if he was shot because he was

258

out after 2200 hours, would we be shot if we attempted to carry him the 200 feet, all exposed to the same tower, to the prisoner's infirmary? (This was in the same building that housed Puett's kitchen very close to our hall.) One of the officers who bunked in the hall and who had served with the lieutenant volunteered to go to the infirmary by a circuitous route that was not exposed to the tower. He did so and, a few minutes later, two aid men brought in a stretcher and carried the lieutenant away. We were told that he died two days later for lack of surgical equipment necessary for removal of the fragmented bullet. (Four months later, I was in Washington, D.C., serving as an Assistant G-3 on the staff of Army Ground Forces when I was asked if I knew anything about this incident. It seems that the Judge Advocate General's office was gathering evidence for the War Crime trials, and that Hans Germann had shot at least two American prisoners and was on the list of those accused for prosecution. I was glad to prepare and sign an affidavit and just hope that it contributed to punishment commensurate with the depravity of Hans Germann's crimes).

On the morning of March 27, 1945, there was startling news from the radio room. BBC had broadcast a rumor that there was a column of the American Third Army that had penetrated the front in the vicinity of Aschaffenburg and was headed east. We knew that this German city was only about 60 miles west of us and wondered if the day of liberation was near. We went outside and searched the horizon to the west, but saw and heard nothing unusual. However, in early afternoon, there was a dramatic change.   First there was a flight of at least three thunderbirds (the town of Hammelburg was in a valley and not fully visible to us) that bombed and strafed the town.   Although we were warned to stay inside our buildings, I used our need for water as an excuse and took the water can to the source of supply on the corner near the latrine where I could see the air over Hammelburg and part of the town, including the railroad yard.   As I was watching the thunderbirds make their repeated strafing runs, two German jet fighters flew over me at low level on their way to meet the thunderbirds' challenge.   (I had never seen a jet airplane before and marveled at their speed and relative quiet in flight).   I wondered if the thunderbirds had exhausted their ammunition on their strafing runs and feared for their survival in the imminent dog fight with these new demons. But the thunderbirds gave as good as they received.   After a brief fire fight, only part of which I could see, I saw two thunderbirds fly westward, and only one German jet flew home.

We soon heard cannon fire and then machine gun fire in the northwest.   The firing continued, moving east and increasing in intensity.   Soon there seemed to be a full scale battle just south of the town.   It was not clear to us what was going on; the radio report concerning deployment of forces that we had heard the day before placed the general American advance facing a line Hanan-Aschaffenburg, west of the Main River.   This was at least 60 miles away; armies did not travel that fast against organized German defenses.

When the light began to diminish in the east, we saw a column of American light tanks and armored cars approaching the oflag from the northeast on the road from Hammelburg. At that moment, we heard the sound of small arms off to the east and saw German foot soldiers from an S.S. camp southeast of the oflag firing on the American column. But their light machine guns and burp guns were no match for the cannon and 50 caliber machine guns mounted on the tanks and the Germans gradually fell back.

It was during this fire fight that Johnny Waters and an Infantry Major who was the appointed Adjutant of the oflag, presumably acting on orders of Colonel Goode, went to the home and CP of the German General Commander. They demanded that the General accompany them to meet the Commander of the American column and surrender the oflag to him. When the General saw how the battle for the compound was developing, he apparently decided that, even in Germany, discretion is the better part of valor. The three officers proceeded from the CP in the direction of the invading column and the American Adjutant was waving a white flag which appeared to be a pillow case or some equally large symbol of truce. Nevertheless, and although the white flag was clearly visible in the dusk to those of us who were watching the action from almost a quarter of a mile away, the S.S. troops fired on the party and seriously wounded Johnny Waters, who fell to the ground (as did the others) until the American tanks dispersed the S.S. culprits.

The Germans withdrew to the south, leaving the ground inside and outside the camp littered with their dead. Waters, who appeared to have been hit in the thigh and hip, and to be in great pain, was lifted to a stretcher and carried to the infirmary near where we were standing. He was followed to the same area by the lead American tank, and an Armored Corps Captain, whose name I later learned was Baum, dismounted through the hatch and announced that he was the Commander of the American reconnaissance in force, which was a heavily reinforced troop from one of the armored divisions of the Third Army. The conversation that followed was shocking to all of us who heard it, because it exemplified the ironies of destiny that are as extraordinary as they are inevitable, in war and in peace.

Captain Baum said, "General Patton gave me a personal order to fight my way to this camp and bring his son-in-law, Colonel John Waters, to him in his CP. Where is he?"

For a few seconds we were all struck dumb. Then someone, perhaps Colonel Cavender, second in command in the camp, said, "But he was the officer who was shot and badly hurt after you entered the compound. He is in the infirmary and I am certain he is in no condition to travel with you."

Then Baum asked that the attending physician be contacted for an opinion and one of the lieutenants left to consult with the regimental surgeon, although we all knew what the answer would be. Before the lieutenant returned, Baum explained that the column had been loaded with extra gasoline and ammunition but had encountered so many road blocks and such heavy enemy fire that they had traveled almost twice the distance of some sixty miles to the point from which

262

they had jumped off for the oflag. As a result of these encounters and digressions, they were virtually out of gasoline and ammunition for the tanks' weapons. When asked about his intentions, he said if there was no gasoline in the camp (we knew of none) he would go west as far as he could and then his men would destroy the equipment, except small arms, and fight their way back to the nearest American forces. It was a daring plan, born of desperation and doomed to failure; there were no friendly troops within at least fifty miles of wooded terrain and icy streams, packed with German armor, artillery and infantry. In fact, it could only have been by a series of major miracles that Baum's relatively small force had reached Hammelburg.

The lieutenant who had been sent to communicate with the attending surgeon returned with the expected report that Colonel waters could not be moved under any circumstances. Thereupon Baum stated that he was moving out, that he regretted that he had no room in his tanks and other vehicles for any of the prisoners of war, but if they elected to ride on top of his tanks or accompany the column on foot they were welcome to do so. This information was passed around to several hundred of the American prisoners gathered in the area and at least one hundred of them opted to leave with the columns, most of them riding on the tanks.

I had made the decision to leave the camp at the moment I saw the lead tank break through the electrified fence, but I didn't like the odds of riding on or walking with a tank that was short on gasoline and ammunition and was sure to come under fire from

German artillery and anti-tank weapons. (In the event they were captured by the Germans the next day after a fierce fire fight about 10 miles west of the oflag.) I was standing with many American officers of the 106th Infantry Division and one Yugoslav officer, my friend, Lieutenant Johanovic.

I said, "I am leaving this camp now, while the Americans still have control of the opening in the fence. I have a compass, and I am going to walk west every night until I find American forces. Does anyone want to come with me?"

There was a long silence and then Major Scales stepped forward and said, "I'm with you." I heard another voice and turned to see my A Battery Commander, Captain Aloysius Menke step forward, asking if he could join us. Then to my great surprise Lieutenant Johanovic said he would like to go. No one else offered, and in any event I considered that more than four men might attract the enemy's attention and would have difficulty in finding concealment during the daytime.

"Let's go boys", I said, and turned toward the break in the fence.

"Wait", said Lieutenant Johanovic, "I know where there is a lot of food from Red Cross packages. We will need it. I'll be back in 10 minutes."

It was actually less than the announced 10 minutes before Johan was seen approaching us with his arms full of boxes of the food typical of Red Cross packages: Spam, cheese, butter, crackers, cookies. But to us it looked like a feast. We divided it up and stuffed it into the pockets of our trench coats. For three of us it would be the only food we would have to eat during the next week.

We followed the last tank through the fence and a feeling of exuberance came over us as we realized that we were at last free, at least when compared with our status during the last fourteen weeks. I felt like shouting with joy, but knew better than to shout for any reason. The American column went west across open ground, but I led our little group through a ravine that ended in a forest about a half mile to the northwest. Once in the forest we found a trail leading in a westerly direction and took it, moving fast through dense trees and underbrush on each side of the path. After about an hour, Johan was panting and asked for a rest. I asked Scales to maintain a lookout to the front and Menke to do the same to the rear. I then sat and talked with Johan, who was still visibly exhausted.

Finally he said, "I am going back to the camp. I will have no trouble finding my way. I have been in prison for 3 1/2 years. I will not be able to keep up with you and your friends. I would be a burden to you. Good luck. I hope I see you again before we meet in heaven." He emptied the food from his pockets onto the ground, embraced me and disappeared in an easterly direction down the trail. The three of us divided the additional food, took time to eat part of it and proceeded west. As I would for seven nights, I led my companions with my illuminated compass in my heavily gloved left hand.

The trail led to a roadway running north and south and, as we frequently would be required to do, we set off through heavy woods and underbrush in a westerly direction. For several hours, we fought the rugged terrain until we reached an area that was only sparsely wooded with crisscrossing paths and an occasional cultivated field. Soon we heard distant sounds that we identified as troops and their equipment and since the first streaks of dawn were appearing in the east, we decided to bed down until darkness again fell.

Because there was no dense forest in which we could all stay hidden throughout the daylight hours, I designated a spot where we would meet when night came, and we each sought an area of trees and underbrush where we would not be visible while we slept. I stopped in light woods with a heavy ground cover of underbrush in which my olive green trench coat would be literally invisible.

I slept until midday when it was necessary for me to crawl from my hiding place to relieve myself. As I was doing so, I heard a noise and looked up to see a German soldier less than 100 feet away. He was short but heavily built, with the insignia of a non-commissioned officer on his uniform and he held a rifle over one arm. He addressed me with a question in his harsh, guttural language.

I had learned some German by listening to the guards in the camp, but I had no idea what the soldier had said. I took a chance and yelled "Ja!", with great assurance.

Then the German said something that I understood to mean, "Are you lost?", and I realized that he had not identified me as an enemy. I shouted, "Nein!", and turned my back, walking away from him in a leisurely fashion. I more than half expected to be shot in the back but nothing happened before I reached a large tree and put it between me and the point where the soldier had been standing. I then stopped, went back to the tree and peeped around it. The German was nowhere to be seen. I resolved to find deeper woods as future hiding places, particularly when I heard the shouts of a German farmer to his mule as they plowed a nearby field. My escape had nearly ended almost before it had begun.

That night Scales, Menke and I met shortly after darkness fell and continued our westerly trek. I tried to avoid well traveled roads, but we encountered a series of villages among small farms. Although it was early evening, we saw no lights, but we couldn't believe everyone was asleep. So through the first two or three of these settlements we crept as noiselessly as possible past the houses. Nevertheless, there was a chorus of barking in which every dog in the village joined. But it would have slowed our progress impermissibly to detour around the clusters of houses.

As we approached the next village, Menke, who as his name suggests had German forbears, proposed that we line up and march through the main roadway. I was dubious but agreed, as did Scales. We lined up and began to march in cadence, trodding as heavily as possible. Not another sound was heard, although this was the largest village we had traversed. As Menke suspected, German dogs were very comfortable with soldiers, but their trained ears were attuned to sneak thieves. Thereafter, we always marched through sleeping villages and no sounds other than our own were ever heard.

Toward morning on this second night we came to a river flowing north and south (probably a tributary of the Main). As had been the case earlier when we had encountered smaller streams across our path, one of us went north and another went south along the bank; we had always found a dam, an abandoned bridge, a shallow ford or a fallen tree that would permit a safe crossing. But this river was at least fifty feet wide, and the only crossing was a highway bridge on which there was an armed guard, an aged German in a heavy overcoat but with a formidable rifle. We had no weapons, not even a pocket knife.

After an hour of searching for another way across the river we held a council of war. I was in favor of approaching the guard in a friendly manner and then rushing him before he could use his weapon, knocking him out and throwing him in the river. The others agreed, but again Menke suggested an alternative. He said if we waited until the guard was on the other side of the bridge and then boldly marched across, he knew enough German to tell the guard we were commandos (the name used by the Germans to designate the enlisted prisoners of war who worked their farms) on the way to work.

"If that doesn't work", he said, "you and Scales can go for his jugular, and I'll go for his gun." Again, it was agreed. We waited until the slow pace of the guard reached the west end of the bridge and then we marched noisily across, with Menke in the lead. The guard took his rifle from his shoulder and pointed it at us. I was relieved to detect that it was an ancient, single shot weapon. As Menke made his explanation,

268

Scales and I appeared to be slouching sleepily at ease. After a moment's indecision the guard waved us on and we lined up and marched off the bridge, turning to the south on a cross road just beyond the river. Whether the guard had second thoughts or was just toying with us will never be known, but when we were about fifty yards from the bridge we heard a shot and the whisper of a bullet just over our heads. As one we jumped into the ditch along the west side of the road. It was three or four feet deep and we were able to bend over and run south through the damp, matted vegetation on its bottom without becoming a target. When we had gone another fifty yards we came to a light forest west of the ditch and sought refuge in the trees. We were not being followed.

We decided that we should call it a night. Again, there was no dense forest so we identified a meeting point and each of us went to find a hiding place. Mine was under two trees that had fallen to the ground against each other, forming a pocket in their intertwined branches. I fell asleep thanking a benign God who had seen me through two close calls in less than 20 hours.

The next night we made very good progress. We found trails and a rutted road through heavy woods that took us generally in the right direction and we were reassured to hear artillery fire a great distance ahead. There were no encounters but we did come upon a stream that we were unable to cross until Scales found a concrete dam, used for irrigation, that provided a perilous passage. We found a dense thicket as a daytime resting place where we all had cover; and for the first time we could designate sentries on two hour shifts, which made the sleeping a great deal sounder.

The next night we again made good progress, although for several hours we fought our way through a heavily wooded valley running generally north and south. The trees and underbrush were apparently virgin growth and there was no sign of human intervention, which seemed to me very strange in a relatively small, heavily populated country which had been inhabited for millennia.

After making our way up the steep western slope of the valley we found an unimproved road that led to the largest town we had so far encountered. We realized that we would be required to find a way to circumvent this densely populated area and that a visual reconnaissance in daylight might prove very helpful. We found a dense copse of trees near the road that would accommodate all of us during the night and, consequently, we stayed together. During my watch, several pedestrians and vehicles went along the road not 100 feet away in the direction of the town. I was glad that none of us snored above five decibels.

I finished my food that day. My last meal consisted of one half pound of butter, made edible only because it was carried in my pocket near my body and, consequently, was not frozen. I surveyed the terrain from the edge of the woods and decided that the most favorable route for our evening trek was to circle the town to the north, starting about an hour after dark in the hope that there would be little or no traffic. At nightfall, the others agreed with this course, and when we deemed that the conditions were favorable, we set out. We met only one person on the woods road we found and followed westbound north of the town. Menke uttered a ward of greeting in German, but there was no response. We left the road for the shelter of the woods and continued west as rapidly as conditions would allow.

The sound of combat ahead of us, artillery and occasional machine gun and rifle fire, became louder as we proceeded, although still at some distance. We also heard the unmistakable sounds of military equipment on the roads,. the changing of metal and the grating of wheels on gravel. We kept distance between these noises and our course, which meant a slowing of our progress as we crept closer to the gun fire. We were careful to find a particularly dense stand of trees and undergrowth for our place of repose for the daylight hours.

Our sleep was more profound that day and it was more difficult for the sentry to stay awake for his two hour stint, an expected result of fatigue and lack of nourishment. The others had finished their rations before I did and had not eaten anything in over 48 hours. Even our canteens were empty because we had not seen a stream or even a trickle of water in the last two nights. I could see a look of desperation in the sunken eyes of Menke and hoped that I was not exhibiting similar signs of panic. We were just entering upon the most perilous period of our adventure and needed clear heads and unfailing resolution.

That night we started early, just after dusk, and after the first hour we stumbled upon a muddy stream in a clearing. Needless to say, we didn't let the sediment stop us from filling the canteens. We stumbled on and soon heard and finally saw German troops and vehicles on a road paralleling our course. To our relief, they were moving to the east, away from the sharp sounds of combat. We continued into a wooded area in which we heard noises reminiscent of our own bivouac areas. We deviated to the south but could tell by the noise of constant activity that we were perilously close to an enemy unit. We now heard firing not only to the west but to the north.

We found a country road that led due west and made good progress until the first streaks of dawn. The woods were sparse on both sides of the road so we separated and sought a sheltered area for much needed rest. I advised each of the others not to stop looking for a place to lie down until they were at least 100 yards from the road. We were to reassemble at dusk at the spot on the road where we separated.

During the day, I slept soundly, but was awakened occasionally by firing of artillery both to the east and to the west and the sound of exploding shells all around us. Sometimes the whine of descending projectiles sounded very near, but there was only one detonation in our immediate area. Some gunner had made an error (called in artillery terms a "short"), and I was glad it was a German; the sound of the falling projectile increased as it came nearer, and reached us from the east. I was also gratified that there was only one round; reassurance that we were merely victims of inadvertence and not an intended target.

We met at the appointed place at dusk, and while I had no mirror for self inspection, I was sure we presented a sorry spectacle. We had all lost between 30 and 40 pounds, and while there was still some muscle, the bones were all much closer to the surface. We had not shaved in a week or eaten in three days. Our faces were sunken and frostbitten, the eyes barely visible. I didn't know whether or laugh or cry, so I did neither.

I said, "We've come too far and have been too lucky to quit now, or to do anything foolish. We are very close; let's keep going." I headed west down the narrow weed covered road and they silently followed.

I could tell after the first three hours that I was near exhaustion. So were the others. We had to stop and rest more frequently, and for longer periods. There was a minimum of talk; we were all saving our breath. But we were rewarded by the fact that we no longer heard firing in the west; the sounds of combat were all in the east. I did not suggest to my companions that we must now have by-passed all elements of the enemy and it would be safe for us to find a highway and stop the first approaching vehicle. I was determined to continue west until some unit of the American armies was sighted, or one discovered us.

When light appeared in the east we were all completely exhausted. There was a thicket of large trees on the south side of the path we were following and we entered it and fell to the ground. After a few minutes of silent gasping for breath, Menke said,

"Colonel, you have done a good job of leading us and I am grateful. But I can't go another day without eating. I am leaving you here and I am going to stop the first person I see and ask for food, whether it is an American, a German or a Russian."

I said, "Good luck. If it is an American or a Russian or anyone but a German, after you have had your meal please come back and get us. We're hungry too."

Menke left without another word. Neither Scales nor I suggested sentry duty. We lay back to back for warmth and each fell into a deep sleep. I have no idea how many hours passed, but we were awakened to the sound of an engine, the beautiful sound of an engine made in America. I looked in the direction of that sound and saw a jeep, occupied by two robust looking American soldiers and Menke. The latter said,

"We've been looking everywhere for you. I thought you had left and we were about to go to the battalion headquarters mess for something for me to eat when something looked familiar to me and it was this forest. Jump in. These guys have promised to feed us."

As I climbed on the rear of the jeep I thought that the sergeant and his driver, smiling at us from their front seats, were the two best looking men I had ever seen. As we drove toward the highway where Menke had contacted them, they explained that their company commander had sent them on reconnaissance to locate elements of the retreating enemy and they had not been able to do so. However, the Germans had been leaving ambushes and road blocks behind them as they retreated and the area could not be considered safe. Relatively thinking, it looked very safe to me.

We learned that we were in the sector of the American Seventh Army and that elements of that Army had captured Aschaffenburg in the last two days and were consolidating for a continuation of their drive to the east (over the ground we had just traversed). We were also advised that the battalion of infantry, to which the sergeant and his driver and the jeep belonged, had captured the town of Hosbach on the day before and planned to continue their advance on the next morning.

When we arrived at Hosbach, we drove to the Town Hall (Stadthaus), which the Battalion Commander had taken over as his CP. It was early afternoon and the Battalion was on hold awaiting orders for the next day. The Commander was a very large and jolly American Major who treated us like heroes to our intense embarrassment; I could never be proud of being a prisoner of war. In our presence, he called the Regimental CP and we heard him say,

"I've got three American officers here who escaped from a prison camp near Hammelburg a week ago, a Lieutenant Colonel, a Major and a Captain, what shall we do with them? . . . No, they're all walking around but they look like scarecrows", winking at us. "All right, it will be done." He then sat down with us while we ate our K rations and said that he had been told to have the Battalion medics check us and, if they said it was okay, to ship us to Corps Headquarters tomorrow.

We thanked him and kept on eating, although we were having difficulty getting our stomachs to accept the quantity of food that our bodies were demanding. We were warned to eat small quantities four or five times a day by the Battalion surgeon, who could find nothing else wrong with any of us, and after too much brandy (which all of the American units were liberating in large quantities) another meal and a good night's sleep, we were on our way to Corps. We had bathed and shaved and were beginning to feel much better about ourselves.

We went through Aschaffenburg on the way to Corps Headquarters and talked briefly to the Colonel in command of the Regiment that had captured the city. He was very tired, but very much in control of the situation. Somewhat to my surprise, he warned that there were still some disorganized German units in the woods between Aschaffenburg and Corps Headquarters, near Frankfurt. Would we never get out of the war zone? But we were beyond fear; we were still unarmed but our driver and relief driver had their rifles and it was far too late to be afraid of anything.

My most cogent memory of the trip to Corps was a stop at a village tavern for lunch. We were utterly without legal tender of any nationality, but somehow our drivers induced the tavern keeper to provide us with a meal; and for the first time in six months I saw an *egg*. In fact, there were two of them straight up on toast. From that moment I knew everything was going to be all right with the world.

And indeed it was. We arrived at Corps Headquarters in mid-afternoon and were told that we would be sent on to Frankfurt and would leave there by air for LeHavre, France, and would go by ship from there to the United States. They permitted me to call the Division Artillery Headquarters of the 106th Division and I was finally able to talk to General McMahon at a camp near Rennes, France, where the Division was being rehabilitated and outfitted.

Still wanting to be in on the kill, I asked McMahon if it would be possible for him to arrange for my return to the Division. After stating that there was a place for me there and he would be glad to have me back (and I prefer to believe he was sincere) he said that the chances were nil. There was a "no exceptions" theater policy requiring all POW's of more than a few days' duration to return to the States for a leave and reassignment or discharge.[8]

When I left Corps Headquarters, fate again smiled in my direction. I was suddenly face to face with two close friends, one a fraternity brother, with whom I had played football at the University of Florida. Dan McCarty, who was to become Governor of Florida, and Julian Lane, who would be Mayor of the City of Tampa, were both on Corps Staff and just happened to be on their way to evening mess. I recognized them immediately, and could excuse their failure to identify me with the same alacrity. Lane wrote his wife that night, mentioning that he had seen me, and when she got his letter, she called my wife with the news. This was only the second time Jean Kelly had received any word concerning me since she was notified before

---

[8] I have since learned that there is also a provision of the Geneva Convention prohibiting the return to combat of former prisoners of war in the same theater of operations as their capture.

Christmas in 1944 that I was missing in action (she had received my first letter from Oflag XIII B, written in January, only a few days earlier).

Frankfurt was almost totally destroyed. The devastation was so complete that I couldn't believe we would be able to find a place to sleep, but our escort took us to a commandeered billet that was damaged but still habitable. After a few days of R and R (rest and relaxation) we were loaded on a DC-3 at an improvised air strip on the outskirts of Frankfurt and transported through Paris, where we stopped only long enough to refuel, to LeHavre, and Lucky Strike Camp.[9]

It was at Lucky Strike that I was informed that of the approximately one hundred POW's who made their bid for freedom on the tanks and in the armored cars of Baum's task force, and the groups aggregating perhaps half that number who took off on their own, only 21 of us reached the American lines. It seems that the reason for such a preponderance of failures was very simple: hunger. After several days of travel during nighttime without detection, most of those who were recaptured made the mistake of approaching farm houses to beg or steal food. The Germans had lived too long in the Nazi police state to let pity overcome their fear of reprisal. So perhaps it was Lieutenant

---

[9] This was one of several areas where POW's and other members of the American military forces were housed (and rehabilitated) while waiting for transportation to the States. Although the accommodations were make-shift, it looked like a luxury resort hotel to us, with three big meals a day and even Red Cross girls.

Johanovic, and his offering of sustenance courtesy of the American Red Cross, who saved us from a similar fate. I gladly give him all of the credit.[10]

My war was over. Although I stayed in the army until after the Japanese surrendered, the remainder of my active duty was in the relative quiet of the G-3 Section of Army Ground Forces at the War College in Washington, D.C. I missed the action of combat; but I certainly preferred missing the action to being missing in action.

Elliott Goldstein

During the period from May 27 till June 20, we conducted live firing drills at a range near Kempernich, Germany located some ten miles from Camp Jones. Starting June 20 and through July 15, the 589th was required to take a series of Army Ground Force (AGF) Tests. These tests are quite comprehensive for an artillery battalion and culminated with battalion test three, a night-firing problem where the artillery fires live ammunition over the heads of its own infantry. Upon the successful completion of all these tests, the battalion was

---

[10] A few of those who found their way into the sector of the Third Army were awarded the Bronze Star, by order of General Patton, who also personally pinned the Distinguished Service Cross on the chest of Captain (then Major) Baum, who was severely wounded before the capture of the remnant of his forces on March 28. These actions by Patton are understandable; but no one has ever been more deserving of the DSC than Baum.

considered qualified to move to the Pacific Theater of Operations for additional combat.

In August the Japanese surrendered and by early September the army decided to return the battalion to the states. Those men without enough points to redeploy home were transferred out of the battalion and high point men from other units took their places. Men of the 589th arrived at Camp Lucky Strike on September 14 and departed LeHavre on September 26 on the *SS West Point.*

After a smooth voyage home, the *West Point* docked at Hampton Roads, Virginia, on October 3. All troops debarked at Newport, Virginia, and were transported by rail to Camp Patrick Henry, Virginia, for processing.

The 589th Field Artillery Battalion was deactivated on October 4, 1945, thereby ceasing to exist as an active unit of the United States Army. But it continued to exist in the minds and hearts of so many of its former members, and others whom it benefited.

When I returned to civilian life, I replied to questions about my army career by saying that I had many experiences but no experience. I was saying that I had encountered and solved many problems, but they had no bearing on or application to my civilian life and profession. I was wrong. I was changed by my experiences, becoming more confident, more willing to accept challenges and believing that anything could be done if I had sufficient determination and was willing to expend the effort. Just as I was changed, and those who served with me were similarly changed, the nation was changed.

The 589th Field Artillery Battalion and the individuals who comprised it were a microcosm of the people of the United States. The United States entered World War II with a tiny standing army, obsolete equipment and ranks of the military filled with citizen soldiers who for the most part had no knowledge of or interest in foreign affairs. The majority of the citizens were similarly disinterested. The United States emerged from the war as a military power whose reach covered the world. The war experience changed the outlook of civilians and soldiers alike. As the individuals changed, so the country changed.

So our experiences, which we thought were unique and personal, were just one facet of the great experience and change that the war brought to the United States. And from that experience, the individuals and the country learned that anything is possible if we are united in an effort to reach a common goal.

John R. Schaffner

When the Germans began their quest to take over the world in 1939, I was fifteen years old. While aware of what was happening, it did not occur to me that I would have a part in this conflict. On December 7, 1941 the Japanese changed my awareness and my concept of the war. I was seventeen and my attitude was, "How dare they do that to us?" I had no conception of either the politics or the consequences of this action; I only knew that "it" happened. And I also realized that I was going to be involved! I had the option to finish high school, which I did, and graduated in February 1943. In March 1943 the army sent me to the 106th Infantry Division at Fort Jackson, South Carolina, where I was assigned to the 589th Field Artillery Battalion. At this point in my life things were so uncertain I did not dare make plans for the future.

After completing the transition from an easy-going civilian life to military discipline, and surviving four major campaigns in the European Theater of operations, I became aware that life offers no guarantee. For too many young boys (yes, we were only boys) life ended in dirty, cold and muddy fields and villages in far distant countries. Being a part of this experience taught me there are things in life that are important while others are not. Through my experiences I learned to tell the difference, and that is the key to having peace of mind.

What kind of person would I have been if there had been no war? Who knows? It didn't happen that way, and I doubt that the war changed me morally. I believe an individual is what he is, no more, no less. World War II certainly changed the world, and our generation changed the outcome of the war. It is hard to imagine what would have happened if the Nazis had continued in power. It is even harder for me to believe what they did while in power, even after having seen it happen.

Arthur C. Brown

Back in the states, Vallie and I were quickly reunited and have lived happily ever after, even to our fortieth wedding anniversary with, at present, a count of eleven in our immediate family to the third generation.

My memories of the army and the war, relived in 1983 on my return to the battlefields and prison camp site, are a part of my life. They were experiences that were not all pleasant, but have added to the fullness of life for me. To some extent my emotions are similar to the thoughts evoked by the old song, "It is better to have loved and lost than never to have loved at all." Except we won.

I now know what the word "hunger" means, the numbing terror of being shot at has been mine, and the importance of "HAVING THE WILL TO LIVE" is not just a bunch of words. I thank GOD that I did survive and was allowed to come back and lead a full, joyful (but at times, tearful) life.

John F. Gatens

I feel our generation contributed a great deal to mankind. The GI Bill gave many of our young people, who could not normally afford it, the opportunity to gain a higher education through college or trade schools. The higher level of education gained by returning veterans produced distinguished professionals, civic and industrial leaders, scientific and medical advances and helped raise the living standards for our whole country.

My personal contribution was well worth the cost. In a small way I helped stop a mad man from taking over all of Europe and possibly the world. We also helped repay Japan for what it did to us at Pearl Harbor and its other transgressions. In combat I may have helped save the lives of friends. I know they helped me to survive as a prisoner of war and to return home safely. Who knows, maybe our combined efforts prevented our having to fight in our own land.

The only regret I have, even to this day, is the grief my family endured when they received the telegram from Uncle Sam saying, "With deep regrets I wish to inform you, etc." They suffered for three months before they were notified that I was a prisoner of war. Now with children of my own, I can imagine what my parents went through.

The World War II years affected me in many ways. I learned to give and take orders. For the first time in my young life I had to assume responsibilities. I became a man in a very short time. At nineteen years of age I found out what the real world was all about. I had to endure the hardships of army life, the dangers of combat, and the horrors of German prison camps. Yes, I became a man in a hurry!

Our group spent almost three years together, much of the time under trying conditions. This fact is what made us close to one another. I believe we are closer together than many brothers. The last time I had seen these fellows was December 23, 1944, at Parker's Crossroads, and I did not see them again until our reunion in 1986. It felt as though we had never been separated. We have stayed very close ever since.

I was delighted when Elliott Goldstein asked us to participate in creating this battalion history. The effort is a heart-warming experience and just one more mission for our group to complete for the major. I just

284

wish we could have written this history years ago when more of our buddies would have been involved.

Randolph C. Pierson

Historians still speculate on various aspects of the Battle of the Bulge. Some refer to this battle as "Eisenhower's Gamble and Hitler's Folly." Historians cannot agree upon the tactical philosophy of leaving the large Ardennes Forest so thinly defended, while amassing enormous military strength on each flank of this area.

One thing historians do agree on is that the Battle of the Bulge, with more than one-half million men involved, is the largest land battle in the history of mankind. Historians also agree that due to the advanced technologies now available to the battlefield, the magnitude of this battle in terms of manpower will never again be equaled.

Reduced to common denominators, the Battle of the Bulge was not a battle for cities; it was a battle for bridges, crossroads, hills, and hamlets. The Battle of Parker's Crossroads was only one of such battles, a battle of men, machines, and weapons pitted against each other. It was also a battle against impossible weather conditions, frigid cold, relentless snow, driving sleet, thawing rain, and deep mud. It was a terrifying battle, and it was personal!

World War II military historians question strategic and tactical decisions made by our nation's highest civilian and military leaders. Obvious blunders were made, but our country prevailed in this war. Quality of leadership is always subject to question. Monday morning quarterbacks, with 20-20 hindsight, will always question leadership decisions previously made under the triple duress of lack of information, insufficient time and overwhelming danger.

The 589th Field Artillery Battalion did not suffer destruction from a lack of competent leadership. It was destroyed because the unit was placed in an untenable combat position, for whatever reason we do not know or question, by higher authority. The quality of leadership and personal courage displayed by Majors Parker and Goldstein are well documented in this history.

However, I would be remiss if I did not point out that even though he was not present at Parker's Crossroads, the influence of our battalion commander, Lieutenant Colonel Thomas P. Kelly, Jr., was deeply felt there. His determination and devotion to the men and officers of the 589th contributed heavily to the commitment to duty we displayed during those five terrible days. The strength of the 589th was forged and tempered by the force and heat of his passion to succeed.

The men of the 589th were a part of the World War II "WE" generation. We learned we could accomplish almost anything through teamwork, initiative, direction, dedication, and desire. With this "We spirit," we became the generation which defeated the Axis war machine and stopped its aggression. This gigantic accomplishment was achieved through courage and teamwork.

After VE and VJ Days, we returned home and applied these same principles to winning the peace. We were more mature and became better educated, thanks to the GI Bill. People of our generation became farmers, merchants, doctors, lawyers, elected officials, entrepreneurs, financiers, engineers, educators, civic and religious leaders. These people built bridges, railroads, skyscrapers and dams. They converted atomic power to peace, deployed personnel and satellites into space. Their farms feed a hungry world.

The ranks of the "WE" generation are growing thin. We are being replaced by other generations; the baby boomers, gen-x and gen-y. The emphasis is shifting from "we" to "me" in these subsequent generations. Whether this shift in emphasis is good or bad is not, and will not be, known for years. All I know is that the emphasis on "we" has a history of producing remarkable results.

I am proud of my generation and its accomplishments. I am honored to have been a member of the 589th team. I wish to congratulate my comrades on a job well done both during and following the trying years of World War II.

When they were passed the torch, they held it high, they carried it well!

John C. Rain

Having been captured at the "crossroads" and having spent some rough months as a prisoner has made me stronger mentally. Now when some unpleasant ordeal faces me, I just think, "Been there--

done that," and face up to it. We did not run; so we did not learn how to run!

Barney M. Alford, Jr.

World War II certainly ruined the good time I was having at the University of Florida. I was young, had no concrete plans for the future, and having fun with my fraternity brothers was important to me.

December 7, and Pearl Harbor, came into the lives of all Americans and their attitudes suddenly changed. I was no different from the other young men of my age; I began to grow up. As the war progressed, lives and evaluations continued to change. I seemed to be able to "go with the flow." The transition from a civilian to a soldier was not difficult for me. As a soldier I still had fun, but now I had acquired responsibilities.

All through the war years millions of other young men grew up and began to assume and discharge responsibilities, just as I did. This maturity, at an early age, defeated the Axis powers, ended aggression, and saved democracy for generations to come. I am thankful we were able to rise to the occasion. We changed the course of events. And we prevailed.

What would the world be like today if we had failed?

Earl A. Scott

In retrospect, I believe our generation showed the world that the greedy appetites of dictators to overrun other nations, enslaving and killing many of the people being invaded, would not be tolerated by freedom-loving nations. Today the United States is the world leader of freedom-loving people. Other nations constantly seek our help in solving internal economic and social problems in addition to assistance in international and intranational disputes embodying the threat of war.

The United States' participation in World War II broke us away from years of economic and social isolation from the rest of the world, to become a part of the world community. We have become a world leader in the community of nations since World War II. The United States is a partner in many international activities and provides leadership in many of them. A prime example of our leadership occurred following World War II. The countries of Europe were devastated, and many of the cities, towns and villages were reduced to piles of wreckage and debris. The United states conceived, financed and administered a plan to restore the European economy and physically rebuild the war-torn infrastructures. This effort, The Marshall Plan, provided new life to Europe.

My personal contribution to the World War II effort was worth the cost. I like to believe my presence and participation, though infinitesimal compared to the total manpower involved in the conflict, contributed in a small way to a successful conclusion of World War II.

The standard Table of Organization for the 589th Field Artillery Battalion included two positions for liaison pilots. I filled one of these positions and

Lieutenant J. Roll Fair filled the other. The pilots, furnished with Piper Cubs, were responsible for providing air observation over the front lines. With the assistance of an observer in the rear seat, targets of opportunity were identified and orders were given to the fire direction center to bring them under artillery fire.

Each soldier, with his unique capability and training, fitted into the whole by fulfilling a particular assignment. With all the parts functioning in the assigned task, it became the full body, operating smoothly and efficiently. I was one of those parts that, together with all the other parts, created the whole body--the Fighting 589th Field Artillery Battalion.

The 589th Group who lived and died experiencing the Battle of Parker's Crossroads were courageous soldiers. They recognized this battle was a life-and-death situation. They saw the living die within their ranks. But the men of this battered remnant of the 589th stuck to their guns and fought valiantly for days until elite forces of the German army finally overwhelmed the crossroads' defenders. This five-day holding action, against battle-hardened German SS troops, was later recognized as one of the major reasons why Hitler's "Grand Plan" had failed.

In reliving the Battle of Parker's Crossroads this group of men bring to memory again the horrible days they endured together during December, 1944. I am certain that as this battle unfolds from their memories after all these years, the concern for each other and closeness experienced during the actual battle are reborn and the comradeship permeating the men in this group becomes even more binding.

I salute these brave men who fought in the Battle of Parker's Crossroads. They were vastly courageous and persistent--not giving up for days until a far superior enemy force overran the small remaining group holding the area with massive manpower and weapons.

The Parker's Crossroads' defenders are true national heroes. They are my heroes too.

Thomas P. Kelly, Jr.

As I have written this account of my experiences from the beginning to the end of my days in combat, including my expense-free tour in the winter wonderland of Central Germany, it has amazed me how full and clear my memory is of events that occurred more than fifty years ago. At first I wondered if I could write an accurate account after so long a time; but one recollection recalled another until I believe that I have remembered and recorded everything of significance that happened in my presence in the four days of December 16 to 19, 1944, the seven days of March 27 to April 2, 1945, and in between. I don't pretend that the conversations are word for word, but the substance thereof is accurately related.

But of all of the memories that tumbled forth when I finally decided to set pencil to paper, the most vivid, and therefore the most troubling, were those of that snow-covered triangle in extreme West Germany and east Belgium where so many boys, who had rapidly reached an early maturity, had lost their lives or bodily functions or their relative freedom. And these memories, once subconsciously suppressed and now fully refreshed, will remain with me forever. It is a Time to Remember.

Since my return to civilization in April, 1945, I have been informed of many exploits during the Battle that I did not witness. For example, I have learned that Cavender held out thirty minutes longer than Descheneaux, and much longer than I thought he could. I have also been informed that a group of infantrymen in the 2nd Battalion of the 422nd did not get the order to surrender and under the command of the Executive Officer of the Battalion avoided capture for an additional two days. But the most heartwarming information that I received after the event was that my 589th Field Artillery Battalion was awarded both the French and the Belgian Croix de Guerre for gallantry in defense of an important crossroad at Baraque de Fraiture, Belgium, by elements of the Battalion that escaped from the Schonberg pocket on December 17. I can only hope that I may have contributed in some small way to the perseverance and courage that soldiers of my Command displayed at that crucial stage of the Battle. They shall always have my admiration and respect.

I was also informed by General McMahon, when I talked to him by telephone on April 3, 1945, that I had been awarded the Silver Star for my part in the Battle. While it is certainly inappropriate, and perhaps even presumptuous, for one to question the merits of such an honor, the mere performance of duty, solemnly undertaken, should not be a basis for special recognition. I saw many, perhaps hundreds, of the members of the 106th Division who gave a great deal more for their Country than I can ever claim to have given, including their lives. But I have no doubt that they went on to an even greater reward.

It behooves each of us to remember that these young, entirely innocent and potentially useful lives need not have been sacrificed. Although given, in most cases, willingly and as a contribution to a great and necessary cause, the reasons that the cause, and the consequent wasting of so many young lives, became essential to the survival of civilization were the satanic evil of Germany's dictatorial cult and the unpardonable complacence and even collaboration of its populace. This is not to say that the majority of the German people condoned the atrocities committed by their leaders. But it cannot be denied, or defended, that a majority permitted this bestial element to take control of the machinery of their government, and to commit execrable outrages in their name that could only demean and denigrate the image of their nation to all other countries of the world.

It was General William Tecumseh Sherman who put the matter succinctly and accurately, when he said, "War is Hell." Similar statements with less brevity and emphasis are attributed to all of the great generals of history, from Alexander the Great to George S. Patton, although some, including Napoleon Bonaparte, Robert E. Lee and Patton, have admitted to a fascination for the intellectual challenge and excitement of combat. Even these great military leaders, however, did not pretend to justify the death, destruction and grief that are the inevitable results of war, even while contending that armed conflict is a commendable test of intellect, courage and character. The deliberate killing or maiming of other human beings can only be justified if it is necessary in defense of one's own nation, or life, or the lives of loved ones. For the foreseeable future on this earth, there will be enough needless, violent death of innocent people without the deliberate training of young persons (of both sexes) for that mission.

For the teaching and training of people to kill their fellow humans is not only debasing but can have disastrous consequences, even if the skills thereby developed are never tested in battle. And if they are, and the individual survives, those skills are even more likely to be utilized for the wrong purposes. To teach that it may not only be right but also simple to kill one's fellow man tends to remove two of the inhibitions to murderous conduct, particularly in persons whose judgment is impaired, of whom there are all too many.

This is not to say that there should not be a standing military establishment who are experts in performing the functions of their profession. Hopefully, there are and will continue to be persons of good judgment, character and motivation who will utilize their skills only under appropriate circumstances. Such evaluations will not always be practical in the exigencies of warfare. And it is precisely to prevent warfare that there must be available in our nation a sufficiently large, superbly trained and equipped military establishment to deter, and if strong enough, to negate any warlike intentions on the part of others. Burglars whose judgment and moral values may be so deformed that they are also potential murderers do not attempt to enter a home that they know is guarded and loaded with booby traps. Even an arsenal of nuclear bombs may be necessary as a deterrent to the Hitlers and Tojos of this world. But what is more important and morally imperative is for us to see to it that there are no more Hitlers or Tojos on this earth, or if there are, that they not be given an opportunity for massive destruction of their fellow man, woman and child.

For it has always been true, as frequently recognized by historians of all nationalities, that all wars, except wars for independence and wars in defense of country are not popular uprisings. Even wars of aggression that are fueled by racial hatreds or religious intolerance have always been the creatures of one man or a group of persons who were determined to give vent to a personal vendetta, innate brutality, overweening ambition, megalomania or a vainglorious egotism. If supported by popular opinion at some time before or during hostilities, that opinion has always been engendered by manipulation and propaganda designed to bring it about, or by a sense of duty to a leader that was induced by that leader's bullying or falsehoods.

Because wars have never been a popular diversion, but are seen by those who must fight them for what they are, evil destroyers of life and everything that makes life worthwhile, it is vital to the elimination of such conflicts that those who are the prospective combatants (and victims) remain in control of the decisions that could lead to war. This requires a democratic form of government in which the electorate retain control of their destiny and not only justifies, but demands, the establishment of some form of democracy as the universal system of government in the world. This can and should only be achieved by education, persuasion and example. Despite disappointments and setbacks, of which there have been, and will be, many, we can now believe that the people of the world are moving in that direction. There are still absolute monarchs and dictators, but their number is diminishing, and so are their unrestrained powers, and concomitantly, the prospect for wars.

But without regard to how we proceed or how it is to be accomplished, it should be obvious that all of us, without limitation as to race, sex or national boundaries, must do everything humanly possible to prevent the recurrence of such activities as those displayed by the Tripartite nations of World War II, and their incredibly evil behavior in the conduct of international affairs. And if the people of any nation should at some future time fail to assume this responsibility, should they not be held fully accountable for their default? At this time in the history of our world, when science, including widespread capabilities in nuclear explosions and germ warfare, has reached a level constituting a constant threat to civilization, do not the moral majority have a right, and a duty, to reject potential disturbers of the peace, and keep government under their control? And if the citizens of any country should fail in this obligation, regardless of the reason, with the result that people of another nation are caused to suffer, should not such citizens be held accountable for their failure, and be required to compensate the innocent for their suffering?

This is not a new concept. Reparations in one form or another have been imposed after many wars, and, unfortunately, not always against the aggressor nation. But there are two new facets to this suggested International Code of Moral Behavior. First, the people of an offending nation should be responsible not only for national depredations, whether or not initiated by its leaders, but also for injury to citizens of another country caused by its nationals, even though their behavior is contrary to the nation's own laws (including acts of terrorism). Second, the Code should be formulated and published so that the people of every nation would have notice of their responsibility before the fact, and so forewarned would be induced and bound to restrain and discipline the potential international criminals in their midst.

It can be argued that any such concept is ahead of the times, but isn't it later than we think? The millions of deaths and crippling injuries suffered by the world's citizens in this century in two World Wars, the Japanese – Soviet and Japanese-Chinese conflicts, the Korean War, the Viet Nam War, the Israeli Wars, Desert Storm and the guerrilla warfare in former Yugoslavia, to name only the major armed conflicts that have caused immeasurable suffering to the people of the world in the last ninety years, should convince us that it has long been time for remedial measures, particularly when it is realized that modern devices of destruction could devastate in a few hours what our Creator has spent hundreds of millions of years to construct for our use and stewardship.

The United Nations is the only organization yet created that has demonstrated that it can legislate in this area and assume responsibility for enforcement. Unfortunately, even the United Nations does not have the support of all of the people on our planet. But conceivably, world opinion can be mobilized in support of such an International Code and can instill validity into its precepts and their enforcement. Is this an expression of hope for a less imperfect world that may some day exist? Or is it a cry of despair from a more imperfect world that may cease to exist? We who inhabit this earth do have a choice, a choice that must be made in favor of a better, safer, happier world, and once made, must be implemented by each of us, and with all of our collective strength and resolve.

About the Author

The principal authors of this brief history of one unbelievably staunch and valiant fighting unit of young American civilians, recently turned soldiers by circumstances beyond their control, are the commander and one of the chief staff officers of that unit. The 589th Field Artillery Battalion, an organic unit of the 106th Infantry Division, not only prevented the invasion of its gun positions by the first onslaught of overwhelming German Forces during the first day of the "Battle of the Bulge", but for many days turned back the attack of full Divisions through one of the main crossroads in Belgium essential to their capturing Antreipt and accomplishing their mission. Both of the leaders of that divinely inspired battalion who collaborated in writing this book were, and unbelievably still are, lawyers practicing in the Deep South.

CPSIA information can be obtained
at www.ICGtesting.com
Printed in the USA
FFOW03n0942270117
31828FF